Divorce Is Only Human

My Journey with God through Divorce

MELANIE BLIEVERNICHT

Ideas into Books® WESTVIEW
Kingston Springs, Tennessee

Ideas into Books®
WESTVIEW
P.O. Box 605
Kingston Springs, TN 37082
www.publishedbywestview.com

© 2009 M Blievernicht, LLC
All rights reserved, including the right to reproduction in whole or in part in any form.

ISBN 978-1-62880-275-7

Second edition, August 2023

Unless otherwise indicated, Bible quotations are taken from the New King James version of the Bible: Copyright ©1982 by Thomas Nelson, Inc.

Every effort has been made to trace copyrights on materials included in this publication. If any copyrighted material has been included without permission and due acknowledgment, proper credit will be inserted in future printings after notice has been received.

Printed in the United States of America on acid free paper.

In honor of the Lord, whose love never fails,

and for the hurting,
that they will find healing through that love.

Table of Contents

Acknowledgements vii
Preface ix
Once Upon a Time… 1
After 3
Emptiness 7
Assumptions 11
Alone 17
Avoiding 21
Work 25
The Torment of Memories 29
Counseling 33
A Cry for Peace 37
Forgiveness 41
The First "Family" Event 45
The Magnet 49
The Nightly Routine 53
Clarity 57
Guilt 61
Back from "We" to "I" 65
My Everything 69
Mutual Friends 73
"Not Yet" Is the Answer 77
Sweet Ana 81
God's Messengers 85
Out of Order 89
Snapshots 93
Stumbling Block 97
The Different Thanksgiving 101
Giving Up the Crate 105
The "In Between" Christmas 109
Slamming Doors 113
Life without a Rear View Mirror 117
Fear-free 121
New Beginnings 125

The Call	131
The Letter	135
Victimhood	139
My Valentine's Date	143
Another Loss	147
Grieving	151
The Shift	155
Trust	159
Today	163
The Journey Continues	167
Epilogue	171

Acknowledgements

Many people have lifted me up over the past several years (what a blessing that they are too numerous to list!). I discovered who my true friends were when life threw something ugly my way, and they remained steadfast with their love and support, none-the-less. I want to thank all of you who reached out to me with your phone calls, notes, emails, hugs, care packages, gifts, shoulders to lean on, and encouragement that "this too shall pass." I also want to extend my heartfelt gratitude to my new friends at Westview. You have given of your creativity, passions, and talents in order to bring this work to fruition. I am so glad the Lord brought us together.

This book is a testimony of God's eagerness to mend our spirits, regardless of the status of our marital relationships, and I'm so grateful that you were part of the nurturing that He provided me through my divorce. I asked God for assistance, and you came to help me with the outside stuff while He did the inner renovation. I appreciate your generosity and willingness to lend a hand or ear. I am a better person for having experienced the TLC you so freely offered. Were it not for the group effort that sustained me over the course of the divorce, I would not be here today with this experience to share. Thank you for your contribution in getting me to this point. I will never be the same, and neither will my relationship with the Lord. You were an important part of that growth and healing.

Love,
Melanie

Preface

Let me start by saying that pain is pain, regardless of how it affects you or when it happens. This book offers experiences, feelings, observations, and prayers that I've had during and after my recent divorce. It is in no way representative of a "typical" divorce, nor do I claim that I have solutions for others with marriage problems. Every strained family dynamic is different, as some involve children or stem from physical abuse or other dangerous circumstances. However, even with the various causes of divorce and the consequent degrees of "nastiness" that can be involved with them, the one thing I want to offer you is hope for your healing and mending your marriage.

My desire is for you to examine your pain and suffering **in the context of your relationship with God** before looking at it as it pertains to your spouse. The Lord has been your constant companion, even before you found your "true love" and got married, and He remains regardless of what happens to your human relationships. He is the only one who can offer healing for you and your spiritual partner, because that sort of medicine only comes from above and within. Every situation is unique, but the Lord is the common connection that binds us to each other. He is our first and final spouse. All we can do is try our best and trust Him to do the rest. Period.

After each chapter, I have left space ("Your Space") in which you can write as an outlet for venting or jotting down your own personal prayers and reflections–whatever you find the need to do. Putting my experience in print has been another type of therapy for me. There is something reassuring about transferring your thoughts to paper to get them out of your system. It may not completely heal your woes, but it can really help. Remember that these thoughts and reflections are just for you, and you can always come back and consider them again later. But also keep in mind that writing is one more avenue through which the Lord may be able to minister to you and answer your heartfelt desire for healing.

In addition to journal space, I have also included a section of Scriptural references at the end of each chapter. These passages have touched me during the divorce process, and I hope that they will do the same for you, whether they offer hope, love, peace, encouragement, or some other form of support. I have kept them handy as a reminder of God's constant presence and desire to comfort me. He wants to be there to do those things for you, too. Most of the passages are cited from the New King James Version (words of Jesus Christ are in bold). I have shown the majority of them in their entirety for easy reference. If you do not have a Bible, I encourage you to get one so that you can highlight passages that have personal meaning for you. God wants us to have an intimate relationship with Him, and the best tool for getting to know Him is His Word. He gives us the wisdom and guidance that draw us closer to Him and shows us how to live healthier and happier lives.

    I also invite you to consider the prompts included with each set of verses. They refer back to the chapter and are meant to help externalize some of the emotional baggage that often gets lugged around after a divorce. Feel free to use them to examine your own experiences. They offer just one more opportunity to unload some of the burden you have been carrying. (Please note: References to divorce may also relate to a separation situation.)

Once Upon a Time...

We met in college, and the more time I spent around him, the more my heart knew that he was set apart from the rest. It wasn't just the lasagna he made from scratch on our first date that impressed me. I savored the conversations that lasted for hours on end, the walks on the beach (sometimes late at night or early in the morning, after marathon cramming for exams), and the entertaining time we spent with his friends. His gifts of poetry and song touched my soul. His very presence made me feel safe, and it seemed that our senses of adventure and confidence were intertwined from the beginning. Most of all, I felt privileged that he had chosen me from the multitudes of women on our campus.

We dated about four years before he proposed in January of 1996, allowing each of us time to graduate and settle into our careers. Eighteen months later we married, and our life together took off. We moved to Atlanta to be closer to my extended family, where I taught and he was in sales – our path was relatively simple. We enjoyed all sorts of new adventures, from taking up kayaking, to camping with our dogs, to doing animal rescue work.

Although we had several career changes and life challenges along the way, I always felt like we could conquer anything with our faith and willingness to persevere through the rough stuff. I loved him like no one else, and I was proud of his amazing character, generosity, and compassion. I had dreams of having a family of our own and watching it grow. He was the love with whom I desired to walk until the end of my days.

His smile and laugh could be infectious. His touch made me melt. His heart was enormous and would reach out to anyone in need, be it a friend or a stranger. He loved to learn and would constantly share all sorts of fascinating facts and ideas with me. On road trips he would have my mind captivated with challenging games of deduction. I remember our long rides in the car, windows down, singing with James Taylor, and his jamming on his harmonica–what I would consider to be some of those moments of happiness that stay with you forever, when all worries feel stripped away. He was a patient teacher, in the martial arts classroom and outside of it. (Lord knows that when we renovated our home, he had many lessons to give me. He showed me how to do everything from laying hardwood floors to hanging drywall, and I learned about the joys of sanding, spackling, priming, and painting.) But he didn't just excel in home project instruction; I felt like he was fantastic at many things.

He taught me about cooking, weapons, history, and language. Even today, I've met very few people who possess a similar variety of interests. He loved my family, and they loved him. He saw most of them pass from childhood into adulthood, watching them marry and start families of their own. He was one of the few individuals that my grandparents invited to be part of the family before he actually was. We loved each other, and I believed in him, regardless of where he wanted to go or what he wanted to achieve. His dreams also became mine, and his happiness and contentment were ever-important to me.

But over the last five or six years, things started to change. The dynamics of the shift are too intricate and intimate to describe, but they have brought me to this moment and have brought you to the beginning of this book. Please know that throughout this entire experience, he has held a special place of love and tenderness in my heart... and he always will.

After

There was no escape. I lay in the guest room bed all night praying that my husband would return to say he was wrong, sorry, desiring counseling... SOMETHING to signify that he didn't mean what he'd said the night before about leaving. Surely, it wasn't over. How was I supposed to work, or eat, or breathe without the man I loved? Everything felt mechanical now. I dragged myself from the bed to the shower, and the hot water didn't even register on my skin. I dressed without concern for coordination or the weather. I didn't eat, though I opened the fridge and pantry in tears, only wishing that the stabbing pain in my chest would go away. My eyes were still swollen from a night of crying, and I had no desire to keep reapplying my make-up. I got in my car and just sat and wept. I wanted to go to work but couldn't. After sleeping in the basement the night before, he had walked by the guest room that morning asking, "Why aren't you going to work?" I stared at him from the bed in shock and disbelief, trying to figure out why he thought that life was just the same as it had been only twelve hours before. Even though I had called in sick last night, I was still amazed that he expected the usual work routine from me. Was he serious?!?!

"We're so sorry," my mom said, as she and my dad listened from their North Carolina home. "You know that whatever you need, we are here. Say the word, and we will be there."

I activated the speaker and put the phone down, trying to contain my moans and tears. But what could they tell me, when there was no remedy for my pain? When I called my best friend half an hour later, her words echoed theirs. As I sobbed, her voice drifted through the receiver.

"Do you need me to come down [from North Carolina]? I can't believe this is happening to you. Oh, sweetie, I am so sorry. What can I do for you?"

Again, no answers came to mind. Within hours, my head and chest felt equally exhausted. I didn't want to leave the house or think or feel. I just wanted to die and escape the pain and loneliness. I wanted someone to shut it all off. I begged God to help me, but the only peace I found is when I literally passed out from lack of sleep. Even then, warped nightmares of our last conversation haunted me, forcing me to relive the helplessness and inadequacy I had felt and once again face the constant barrage of blame for not meeting any of his needs. I had nothing in my possession that meant anything to him... not my efforts, my heart, or my devotion. I especially did not have whatever solution he was expecting to fix all of our problems. In his eyes, it seemed like I was now unnecessary and inconvenient.

I went into the bathroom to throw up, but nothing came out but more wails and convulsions. I sank onto the floor and curled up, silently pleading with God to help me–to help us. But no answer came. I tried to keep convincing myself that horrific things like this just didn't happen to me. I don't know how long I was there, but eventually I sat up and got slowly to my feet. I glanced in the mirror, not recognizing the face that stared back at me. I wished that there was something I could have done to prevent my suffering, and I dreaded each new minute of pain with no answers or relief in sight.

Lord, what do you expect of me now? What am I supposed to do?

Your Space

AFTER

*"Naked I came from my mother's womb, And naked shall I return there.
The LORD gave, and the LORD has taken away; Blessed be the name of the LORD."*

Job 1:21

*"Do not hasten in your spirit to be angry, For anger rests in the bosom of fools.
Do not say, 'Why were the former days better than these?'
For you do not inquire wisely concerning this."*

Ecclesiastes 7:9-10

Have you ever been "left over" from a relationship? What went through your mind?
___
___
___
___

Did you find any answers in the midst of the break-up?
___
___
___
___

Emptiness

I feel completely hollow inside. I am a shell of the vibrant and excited spirit I used to be. My mind counts the moments passing very slowly, as if affirming each second and its marking of time passed *without him*. The void is so vast that it overwhelms me. My soul cries out to the Lord to rescue me from this plight, as if He will swoop down and carry me away to a pain-free paradise. But my pleas are met only with silence. So I remain in this place alone, with the darkness pinching, scratching, and burning at the edge of my awareness. It follows me everywhere. I walk through the house that used to be a home, and the memories in each room exacerbate the absence of companionship and love. I wander into the closet to sniff the remainder of his clothes, seeking comfort in his familiar scent. But it flees from my nostrils, taking with it the hope of a temporary bandage for my wounded heart.

My life has become like a funeral parlor... a place that signifies death... only without friends and family standing about reminiscing with fondness and laughter, and without understanding and closure for my heart and soul. I am lost in this abyss by another's choice. Death would be at least the result of natural order, but to feel like a widow by his decision leaves me adrift in an endless sea of heartache. Oh, God, where do I go now? I am desperate to figure out what is real these days. I once had illusions of happiness and dreams come true, but they have been replaced by excruciating pain and the sense that I have been permanently discarded.

Please come and be with me, Lord, that I may one day feel like I have value and purpose again.

Your Space

Your Space

EMPTINESS

"For He satisfies the longing soul, and fills the hungry soul with goodness."
Psalms 107:9

"... The effectual, fervent prayer of a righteous man avails much."
James 5:16

Where do your greatest feelings of emptiness come from?
_____
_____
_____
_____

How has divorce created emptiness in your life?
_____
_____
_____
_____

Have you been able to heal from some of that emptiness? How?
_____
_____
_____
_____

Assumptions

As I wondered when this horrible week would end, I began to accept the reality that my life was probably headed towards a divorce. I had tried to convince myself that our marriage was still salvageable, but the longer he was gone and out of contact the more I began to question whether our relationship could be healed. Sure, he said he needed time and space, but what was there that he needed to figure out, and why wouldn't he take me up on offers of counseling? Although I continued to offer whatever concessions I could in order to maintain a dialogue with him, my mind whispered that my efforts were probably for naught. I thought that I had a reasonable understanding of the causes of divorce, but as I looked around me at people in divorce situations, I realized that God had already begun correcting my preconceived notions about this process.

For instance, I thought that the husband and wife were equally responsible for causing the divorce, and that the separation was a mutual decision. However, this was not the case when I talked to family, friends, and even casual acquaintances. I also used to believe that infidelity was at the heart of most divorces. Though some people shared with me that their situations related to affairs, others claimed different factors to be responsible. In addition, I thought that I would know only a few people here and there who had been through a divorce. But when I became aware of the possibility of divorce in my own life, people appeared out of nowhere to share their own experiences with me... even those I've known for years but who never mentioned that they had previously divorced. Furthermore, I saw a large percentage of broken marriages as a reflection of their "just not trying hard enough." However, now having stood on the brink of this reality, I reflected on my own exhaustive efforts and recognized that this belief was also not true. Previously, I had convinced myself that each person had choices in the state of their union. But my conversations with others, as well as my own history, demonstrated that some choices could be taken away. Lastly, I believed that only a small percentage of people were in dangerous relationships and needed divorce to keep them safe. Yet, over the last couple of years, I recalled several personal accounts from friends and acquaintances regarding abuse and harm inflicted by their ex-spouses. It seemed like God had continued to remind me that life was not always a matter of how I chose to see it, and I needed to put my judgments behind me.

While talking to the numerous people that God has put in my path, I found that the commonalities were sad but not surprising. They came from divorced family, friends, and acquaintances as well as those in marriages that seemed to be collapsing. Some of the characteristics they shared with me included, but are not limited to:

1) Lack of commitment to the Lord as a couple

2) Issues, both individual and as a couple, that have gone unchecked (no communication about the "nitty-gritty" stuff)

3) One or both spouses in a constant state of frustration, depression, anger, or a combination of these

4) Lack of general concern for others in the home (whether spouse, children, or both)

5) Absence of Christian accountability partners (outside of the marriage) that hold each spouse's behavior to a standard of the community (i.e. – men's group, women's group, close friends, etc.)

I was shocked by how much I identified with these characteristics. So, I took that list and decided to make one of my own–one that I could use to remind myself of ways to keep my relationship with my spouse on a healthy track. Although we had obviously hit a deep pothole in the road of our marriage, I hadn't given up and would continue to try and find tools that could help us resolve our issues and mend our hearts. (I have also included Scriptural references that came to mind while I was compiling the list.)

1) For true spiritual contentment and a healthy, strong marriage, God must come first for both spouses (individually and jointly). (Ephesians 5:22-33)

2) Everyone in the home is responsible for modeling his or her behavior after God's Word.

3) Both spouses need to find an amicable way to discuss their problems, even if a neutral third party (counselor or mutual friend) has to assist them. Tucking issues away makes them grow and become even more toxic. (1 Corinthians 13)

4) If you surround yourself with people who encourage you to behave in a manner contrary to your morals, values, and beliefs (in relation to God and family), you can expect your life to follow that same route, so keep the company of those who encourage your Christian walk.

5) Family members need to find a way to balance work/school/play/friends/rest in a way that consistently prioritizes faith and family above all else. (no excuses)

6) Each spouse needs to seek out one or two trusted confidants who will help them stay "in check" with God, themselves, and with their loved one when times get rough. These friends are there to keep them focused on what's important and to discourage impulsive and unhealthy decisions and actions. (2 Timothy 2:2)

As I finished this passage, I saw gaps in my marriage that I wished I'd been able to address years ago.

If anything, God, please help me to remember these lessons so that I don't repeat any of my mistakes in the future. And I also promise to stop making casual judgments about things like divorce. You've made me aware of how little I actually know.

Your Space

Your Space

ASSUMPTIONS

"Trust in the LORD with all your heart, And lean not on your own understanding;
In all your ways acknowledge Him, And He shall direct your paths.
Do not be wise in your own eyes; Fear the LORD and depart from evil.
It will be health to your flesh, And strength to your bones."

Proverbs 3:5-8

What was your first experience with divorce?

_____
_____
_____
_____

How did the experience compare to the ideas you previously had about divorce?

_____
_____
_____
_____

Did you learn anything that you feel might be important to share with others?

_____
_____
_____
_____

Alone

It's been two weeks since he left, and the saddest part of my situation is realizing that I have been alone in our marriage for years now. I could not compete with his all-consuming business, nor did I have four paws and a cute little tail to wag to get his attention. My presence no longer drew his interest. I am beyond being physically alone; I have been completely isolated from him in all ways except legally. It's the worst pain and loneliness I have felt in my life. I desire what I cannot have, and he shows no initiative in trying to save our marriage. I would do anything to help us, if he would just say the word. Now, I continue to eat alone, sleep alone, do yard work alone, repair the house alone, pray alone, and cry alone... with no promise of change.

My mind wanders to possible explanations. Is there someone else? Is this a mid-life crisis? Could it be some weird symptom of addiction? Even with these thoughts running through my head, my heart tells me that it is something much deeper and not as easily distinguished–a matter of the spirit.

I am overwhelmed by the feeling of helplessness: I realize that there is absolutely nothing I can do to save this relationship. He will not let me back into his world, which makes me a woman who has been cast aside. Fortunately, I have a friend coming into town to visit next weekend who will bring me love, hugs, and reassurance that life will go on. At least I won't be alone, like when I suffered through another Mother's Day without children of my own... again. Then there was Father's Day with no husband, followed by our eleven year wedding anniversary, and my birthday wrapped up that two month window of what used to be my life. Even days that don't represent a celebration of some kind seem to crawl by at a snail's pace. Now he has stopped sending emails and calling me to check and see how I am. I no longer warrant the loving attention I did years ago.

Trying to fill in any gaps in time, I spend my days at work, Bible Study, and church, always surrounded by people, yet feeling completely alone. Everything makes me cry, from music to commercials, billboards, bumper stickers, and couples walking hand-in-hand. I feel like no one understands. I know God is with me, but my body aches for a physical person to hold me, love me, and laugh with me. I want someone whom I can love, care for, and have a family with, since my insides are telling me that he is never coming back.

The truth is not that his leaving made me *more* lonely (than when we lived under the same roof), but it demonstrated his desire to be free of me. And no matter how much I believe in saving our marriage, this complete rejection forces me closer to divorce. His words echo in my mind.

"You're not meeting my needs."

Well, how can I when you don't come home during waking hours?

"You just don't understand."

Then, please tell me or we can talk about it in counseling.

"When I have the money and a place to go, I'm gone."

What?!?

Lord, PLEASE intervene and show him that You are all-powerful and can help us. PLEASE miraculously mend our union so that we can come together again. PLEASE do not dismiss the love and devotion I have for this man. I know You can overcome all things. Please take my loneliness away and fill me with the peace of Your presence, and I beg You to do the same for him.

Your Space

ALONE

"Be anxious for nothing, but in everything by prayer and supplication, with thanksgiving, let your requests be made known to God."

Philippians 4:6

"For we do not wrestle against flesh and blood, but against principalities, against powers, against the rulers of the darkness of this age, against spiritual hosts of wickedness in the heavenly places. Therefore take up the whole armor of God, that you may be able to withstand in the evil day, and having done all, to stand."

Ephesians 6:12-13

Has being alone brought you closer to the Lord or pushed you away? How?

_____
_____
_____
_____

What do you do to help you feel less alone? How long does that feeling last?

_____
_____
_____
_____

Avoiding

It seems like depression follows me everywhere. Even though I know some of my family and friends see it, I spend most of my time and effort trying to hide it. But how can I? I get dressed in the hallway to avoid his stuff in the closet. I sleep in the guest room to avoid our bedroom. I dodge people at the store so that I don't have to fend off their questions about how he is doing. I avoid our restaurants and hang-outs so that I don't have to explain that there is no "we" anymore. I cringe when I open mail from mutual friends who are oblivious to our situation – I decide not to call and tell them. I duck family events because even hugging makes me want to cry. I keep conversations with my church family as shallow as possible for fear of drowning in my sorrow. I avoid my neighbors because I am alone, see myself as a failure, and feel guilty about not being able to keep my yard up to par. When the phone rings, I screen the caller ID so I don't get sabotaged with an expected meltdown, should an unsuspecting friend or relative call. I keep all of my lights turned off at night to discourage anyone from coming by unless they know I am home. I try to avoid being home when I know he will be by to put our dog Ana outside... a sad irony, considering how many nights I would have given anything to catch a glimpse of him. Since I can't escape the pain of my situation, I even take up drinking for a week or so to avoid having to think or feel.

I used to believe that I had so much to offer others, but now the only thing living within me is heartache and despair–nothing of value to anyone. I have no reason to do, go, be, or whatever until I can move beyond this point of valuelessness. Even my dogs seem confused as to why I am so different than I used to be, but thankfully they love me anyway. I am tired of manipulating my steps to avoid the ongoing grief that hits me everywhere I go.

Lord, please, please, take it all away or show me what I can do. I am tired and completely discouraged. I have tried to use many things to kill the pain, but what I thought could be used as tools for relief only dulled the pain. They didn't address the cause of my grief in any way. I know that I can't control my pain, but I don't want it to control me either. Please rescue me. I don't ever want to start avoiding You, and I desperately need Your help.

Your Space

Your Space

AVOIDING

*"Blessed be the God and Father of our LORD Jesus Christ,
the Father of mercies and God of all comfort, who comforts us in all our tribulation,
that we may be able to comfort those who are in any trouble,
with the comfort with which we ourselves are comforted by God."*

1 Corinthians 1:3-4

"I will lift up my eyes to the hills – From whence comes my help? My help comes from the LORD, Who made heaven and earth."

Psalms 121:1-2

Have you been forced to dodge people, places, and correspondence because of divorce? Which situations were the most difficult? Why?

_____

_____

_____

_____

What happened after you avoided those situations? Did they keep popping up or eventually go away?

_____

_____

_____

_____

Work

My only waking reprieve right now is work. It's been a month since he left, and only my boss and a couple of coworkers know my situation. I don't know what I would do if I didn't have to go to the office each day, if I didn't have lists of things demanded of me on the job. Each time I hesitate or lose focus on the task at hand, I have an anxiety attack. I sneak back to the stockroom or bathroom, quietly close the door, and weep. I avoid talking to others about anything personal. I slip out as soon as it is 5:00p.m.. I hope they don't think me rude, but I couldn't possibly survive the office gossip mill, should the rest of them find out what is going on. I cling to the stability and routine of my position and responsibilities, hoping that they will preoccupy my mind long enough to stop the hurting, even if for only a few minutes at a time. I don't want to take time off because my back treatments (prolotherapy to rebuild my ligaments that were damaged by a serious injury) use up all of the time off I accrue, and now I have no idea what else is coming. What if he chooses to divorce me? What will I do? How will I get up each day? Will I be able to work? Will I lose my job because I can't function? How am I supposed to cope with possibilities I've never before faced? *God, what will You do to help me?*

I am grateful for my boss. She is there for me, whether I need to vent or take time off. I'm sure she, too, wonders what will become of me.

"Melanie, if there is anything you need, just let me know."

My few coworkers who are aware of the situation also extend invitations.

"Do you want to come over and spend the night?"

"How about joining us for dinner?"

"Want us to go find him and straighten him out?"

"We will do whatever we can to help... whatever you need."

I feel like I *need* to go permanently numb in order to survive this living hell. *Lord Jesus, what good will come of this?*

God, I have worked so hard for much of my life, and now I'm struggling to simply hang on. Please give me peace at work, that I may temporarily escape the torment of what used to be my loving home and marriage. Let me find comfort in the presence of my coworkers and remember that they also have challenges and pain for which they need my reassurance. Thank you for preparing this place as a safe harbor for me, at a time when I feel lost at sea and nauseous from the swells of heartache. Somehow, Lord, please make me the better for it. I am tired of suffering, but I will endure it because I trust You to end it and salvage what is left of my spirit. Please use my work place in that healing. I never thought I would be so needy and fragile, and I pray You will bring me through this quickly so that I may be effective both to my office family and for Your work. I have not forgotten why I am here. I'm just so tired of working two jobs—earning a living and surviving this devastation. Please overwhelm me with my job so that the pain will be pushed aside, at least until I am able to deal with it.

Your Space

WORK

"Because you have made the LORD, who is my refuge,
Even the Most High, your dwelling place, No evil shall befall you,
Nor shall any plague come near your dwelling;
For He shall give His angels charge over you, To keep you in all your ways.
In their hands they shall bear you up, Lest you dash your foot against a stone.
You shall tread upon the lion and the cobra, The young lion and the serpent
you shall trample underfoot. Because he has set his love upon Me,
therefore I will deliver him; I will set him on high, because he has known My name.
He shall call upon Me, and I will answer him; I will be with him in trouble;
I will deliver him and honor him. With long life I will satisfy him,
And show him My salvation."

Psalms 91:9-16

Have you used work to distract yourself from the pain of divorce?

_____
_____
_____
_____

Do you feel safer when you have a "to do" list to keep you pre-occupied? How does this affect you during the time(s) when you don't have a planned activity?

_____
_____
_____
_____

The Torment of Memories

Even though I am now alone, I am stalked by all of the memories. Most used to be images that brought warmth, happiness, and laughter, but now they haunt me. This has been especially difficult because I am naturally an emotional being, clinging to pictures and stories recounted many times over. These recollections are now fighting constantly for my attention, morning, noon, and night. They keep drawing me back to the places and times that touched me deeply... a kind word *from him*, a tender touch, a slow dance... the snapshots of joy that used to sustain me whenever we were apart.

But since he left, they are like razor-sharp knives to my soul. Instead of providing comfort, they sucker-punch me in the gut, as if there is a little voice saying, "Don't you remember when he used to (do this)(say that)(love you)?!?" One image links immediately to another so quickly that sometimes I literally say "No!" or "Stop it!" to try and control the onslaught of torment. I feel like the enemy is manipulating my situation to kick me while I am down, and I fight hard to keep my anger at bay and my brain focused on what God promises to do for me, instead of what my husband has not. Unfortunately, I am so tired every day now that my emotional energy is depleted, and I have a hard time concentrating on any task at home or work. (At least my driving has been okay... due to God's protection, I'm sure!)

I pray for the armor of God regularly, but maybe I cannot defend myself because the Lord is using this window of my life to start the healing process. I can't imagine how, but I have to embrace the trust I have in Him, or I would go completely mad. It's like going to the doctor and having blood drawn: as soon as the needle hits your skin and dives down below, all time seems to stop. So there you sit, trying to keep breathing through the pain, wondering "How much longer?" but knowing that there is a clear reason for the process, and that you will probably be better off for it. Then, after an insane period of time, it is finally over, and you can look back on the experience and see that it was actually shorter and more tolerable than you thought. However, when you are in the thick of it, everything feels much worse than anything you can imagine. Without the Lord to carry us through, we would crumble back into dust, never to be made whole again.

God, I'm counting on you to make something beautiful of my misery, because only You can. Keep me together so that I can come out on the other side of this part of my life and tell people, "Look what my Lord did for me."

Your Space

THE TORMENT OF MEMORIES

"... we also glory in tribulations, knowing that tribulation produces patience; and patience, experience; and experience, hope."

Romans 5:3-4 (KJV)

"Only be strong and very courageous, that you may observe to do according to all the law which Moses My servant commanded you; do not turn from it to the right hand or to the left, that you may prosper wherever you go. This Book of the Law shall not depart from your mouth, but you shall meditate in it day and night, that you may observe to do according to all that is written in it. For then you will make your way prosperous, and then you will have good success. Have I not commanded you? Be strong and of good courage; do not be afraid, nor be dismayed, for the LORD your God is with you wherever you go."

Joshua 1:7-9

When you look around now, does your world feel smaller because of divorce?

_____
_____
_____
_____

Are there certain places or memories that hurt you more than others? What are they? Why are they so powerful?

_____
_____
_____
_____

Counseling

I went to my first counseling session this morning. Since he refused to go with me, I decided to go by myself, without telling him. I feel like if he knew, he would further blame me in some way, as if my acknowledging the need for counseling was a personal strike against his character. All I know is that the decline of our marriage feels like it is being placed squarely on my shoulders, and I refuse to give up. As I sat before my therapist, I began to recount the pain that had brought me to this point. She would ask a question, and I would respond, hoping for some insightful feedback or strategy.

"Why do you think you are here?"

To try and save my marriage.

"When did you feel like things started to go downhill?"

I don't know exactly. I was too busy scrambling to try and take pressure off of him and do what I could to support his endeavors. Does that sound like an excuse? So when exactly did my perspective slide so far off-center?

"What do you believe you can do now that will make a difference?"

I have no clue. I am out of ideas and feel like a complete failure.

I am an action person; I simply need to figure out what needs to be done and do it. The fact that I was seeking counseling was a testimony that the ideas and creativity of my family, close friends, and relationship books had not worked; and I had already exhausted myself before the Lord in prayer, every single day without apparent progress. This was the only avenue (other than magazine articles and commercial pitches) that I hadn't tried. I had done everything else I could think of, from changing my clothes and shoes, to picking out new perfumes and lotions, upgrading my make-up, having my fingernails and toenails done regularly, cooking different meals, giving him gifts, helping out with his business whenever I could, and whatever else I thought might generally get his attention and convey my love for him.

So I sat before her, asking for some light to be shed on the missing link that would save my marriage. But it was never revealed. She affirmed my efforts but found it difficult to think of a suggestion that was new. I felt better after the session, but I didn't have any answers or additional hope.

My next appointment is in two weeks. I pray that the Lord will show me what to do in that time. I am so tired of trying to figure it out all by myself.

Please, Lord, do not make me wait for change, if there is something you would have me do. Just show me and consider it done. My heart would not be able to take sitting on the sidelines only to watch a losing battle.

Your Space

COUNSELING

"Let all that you do be done with love."

1 Corinthians 16:14

"Judge not, and you shall not be judged. Condemn not, and you shall not be condemned. Forgive, and you will be forgiven. Give, and it will be given to you: good measure, pressed down, shaken together, and running over will be put into your bosom. For with the same measure that you use, it will be measured back to you."

Luke 6:37-38

Have you and/or your spouse gone to see a counselor? What happened? Did you continue to go?

_____
_____
_____
_____

Do you feel that the counselor was able to help you (or both of you)? Why or why not?

_____
_____
_____
_____

If you did not seek counseling, what was your reasoning? How do you feel about that decision now? Do you think it would have made a difference?

_____
_____
_____
_____

A Cry for Peace

For two months I have tried to rationalize what can be done to save my marriage. I am obsessed with replaying the last several years in my mind to figure out what I could or should have done differently that would have changed the state of my here and now. I have identified some of the culprits but can't seem to amass them into enough to warrant a divorce, and this morning I awoke extremely angry. It came out of nowhere.

All of a sudden my insides seethed with fury for the circumstances in which I found myself. I was angry at him for shutting me out for so long and refusing to engage in healing our marriage. I was angry at being abandoned, for being yoked with so much debt only to be deserted, for being given what felt like no choices, for only an occasional email to make sure I was still breathing, for no help with the house/chores/bills, for all of my energy, love, and devotion that now amounted to nothing. I was angry at myself for not demanding more answers for his change in behavior, for his obsession with his work, for not pursuing my own dreams and passions in order to pursue his, for putting all of my waking energy outside of work into him but with no thanks or acknowledgment, for not holding him accountable for us and our relationship with God before everything else, for believing that if I just prayed hard enough and long enough that everything would be okay. I was angry that I had a physical injury that I felt made me less attractive to him. I was angry with myself for wasting so much time waiting and believing that I could actually make a difference in the state of our relationship.

The flames of passion licked at my soul, melting away the buffer of restraint that had kept my anger at bay. I got swept up in outbursts of screaming and crying. At times, my blood pressure got so high I didn't want to talk to anyone for fear I wouldn't be able to contain myself. I threw and shredded things. I yelled at the top of my lungs. I destroyed belongings that used to be dear to my heart.

I didn't talk to God much that morning, except to say that I was sorry that He had to listen to the slew of rage-filled thoughts and mean words that came out of me. I'm not sure how many times I exploded–it happened over and over again. I remembered family and friends telling me that the anger would eventually pop up as a natural response to pain and healing, and I had waited for it to rear its head, which it did full force. I had little energy left before it arrived, and it seemed to jack me up so high that I felt like I was crashing on the way back down.

I know that anger is a necessary part of getting through times when you feel like you've been wronged. But God, please get this out of my system so I can pull myself out of the emotional gutter and make You proud of who I am and who I will be after all of this. I don't want you to think any less of me.

Your Space

A CRY FOR PEACE

"So then, my beloved brethren, let every man be swift to hear, slow to speak, slow to wrath; for the wrath of man does not produce the righteousness of God."

James 1:19-20

What particular aspect of your divorce situation makes you most angry? Why?
_____
_____
_____
_____

Do you have any power to change your situation?
_____
_____
_____
_____

Do you have any ways to externalize your anger in a healthy fashion? What are they?
_____
_____
_____
_____

Forgiveness

I'm starting to see, from the unanswered phone calls and emails, that he has no intention of ever coming back. After trying to survive many weeks in limbo, I feel absolutely paralyzed with the impending doom of divorce upon the horizon. It's like I've wandered into a marsh, sunk down far enough to be stuck, and am simply waiting for the tide to come in and do away with me. There are so many feelings all muddled together in my head and heart, sometimes just lying there and other times thrashing about looking for an escape. They are impossible to target and deal with because no single emotion will separate from the rest in order for me to address it. I am weary and overwhelmed. I've been praying on our situation for what seems like forever, and if God is answering, I must not be listening well enough to hear. But, I still trust Him to guide me, even when I'm distracted and hurting.

Since I wasn't getting any nudges (that I could tell), I took the perspective of the Word and what God expected of me as a wife, even though my husband didn't look at me that way anymore. What could I do for him? I had been praying for us, but I redirected those thoughts towards him alone. Since I knew he was leaving, I began going through the house, gently cleaning his things and packing them safely away, labels and all. I even sorted through our old boxes in the attic and basement to make sure I hadn't accidentally kept anything of his. But I felt a little stab of pain from each item I packed bearing a memory and a piece of my heart, and I cried a lot.

As I made my way through the closets, cabinets, and eventually to the garage, I tried to stay focused. I kept asking the Lord, "What more can I do? What more can I give?" When the task was finished and I had stopped to rest, I recognized something that had yet to be done. God showed me that I needed to forgive my husband. I had to find a way to put aside all of the obvious drama of the situation, reach deep down, and let it go... let him go. I wasn't condoning what he'd done, but without releasing my pain and anger, I was preventing God from having full access to me. I was blocking the Lord from bringing me the healing and peace that I so desperately needed and for which I had prayed.

So I sat on the floor, closed my eyes, and asked Jesus to help me find the strength to forgive him–not just saying it, but truly meaning it–no strings attached. I was there for a long time, and forgiveness didn't happen all at once. However, I was able to grasp the edge of it, like the corner of a tablecloth whipping in the wind across a picnic table. Again, that night beside my bed, I revisited the forgiveness request and was able to release a little bit more of the pain and anger. After several days of serious focus and prayer, God helped me fully grasp that tablecloth and toss it freely into the sky to be carried away on the breeze. The sensation was tremendous! The pain that I'd experienced in my heart and mind seemed lessened almost immediately. My hope grew, and the Lord created a protective buffer that began to distance me from the unhealthy aspects of my waning relationship with my husband. I felt like God had begun to form me anew. I knew that no matter what happened from this point on, I was going to be okay—no, better than okay, because I would always have the Lord, and He would always have me.

Your Space

FORGIVENESS

*"Remember, O LORD, Your tender mercies and Your lovingkindnesses,
For they are from of old. Do not remember the sins of my youth,
nor my transgressions; According to Your mercy remember me,
For Your goodness' sake, O LORD."*

Psalms 25:6-7

"And whenever you stand praying, if you have anything against anyone, forgive him, that your Father in heaven may also forgive you your trespasses. But if you do not forgive, neither will your Father in heaven forgive your trespasses."

Mark 11:25-26

Who is the person that hurt you the most in your divorce? Is there more than one person who injured you and needs your forgiveness?

_____

_____

_____

_____

Have you been able to forgive your ex for whatever pains he/she inflicted? If so, how? If not, why not?

_____

_____

_____

_____

Why do you think that forgiveness is so much harder than some of the other aspects of divorce?

_____

_____

_____

_____

The First "Family" Event

Even though the Lord had put forgiveness in my heart, I continued to face emotional obstacles in my daily life. By the end of the third month, I ran into my birthday – a hard twenty-four hours. The card and gift certificate he left me felt contradictory to the tide of pain and change that he had caused in our relationship. So having survived my birthday weekend without him (thanks to many loved ones who came to visit with tidings and hugs), I looked forward to the next weekend's baby shower. My cousin's wife was due in several months, and this shower was to celebrate the new branch to be added to our family tree. What was once an event I anticipated with excitement and glee had become an ominous hurdle. I had tried to shy away from events involving my extended family because it became harder and harder to make excuses to my aunts, uncles, and cousins as to why I was always alone. The shower would be my first get-together with my family where everyone would already know that he had left me. It wouldn't be just another gathering where I was solo without reason... again.

I couldn't bring myself to shop for baby stuff, since my heart was too devastated to even think about my own family that would never be. The days dragged by until it was finally time for the party. I didn't care about my wardrobe or hair, but I managed to look presentable. I got lost on the way in the dreariness of the rainy day, and I pulled over to cry in an empty parking lot. How was I going to survive the rest of my life, if this was how miserable I was on the way to seeing a huge group of people so dear to my heart? I felt like part of my soul had been amputated.

I finally got to the house and focused very hard on putting whatever wall of strength I could muster up to greet my loved ones. *Grandma, I sure wish you were here to protect me from the loneliness and the feeling that I'm suddenly a fifth wheel,* I thought. But Grandma, who had been the sweet and dear matriarch of our family for many years, had moved on to be with her true love in heaven. So I would have to take this significant step on my own. I did everything to avoid the eye contact that accompanied hugs from my relatives–those looks that screamed out understanding, compassion, and sorrow, yet went unspoken in the current setting of celebration.

I was able to keep myself in check by prompting everybody I spoke with to tell me more about the goings-on in their lives. But as the presents were being opened, and the voices dwindled, and husbands pulled their wives close to share a smile and a kiss, I completely lost it. I casually tucked myself into a corner of another room, out of sight and hearing range, and I sobbed quietly with only the Lord to keep me. I could not defend myself from the memories, hopes, and broken dreams that suffocated me in the stillness of my cousin's dining room. I leaned against the wall for support and tried to stifle my anguish. The last thing I wanted or needed was to be "the scene" everyone remembered from the day's activities. In the middle of my struggle, my cousin (the hostess) came around the corner looking for something. She saw me, came over and hugging me tightly, kindly whispered, "I think it was very brave of you to come alone today." She gave me an extra squeeze and was off again with candles and matches in hand.

    I will never forget that moment as long as I live. Her sweet words somehow gave me the courage to stick it out and not secretly flee the party in my grief. Eventually, I was able to drift back into the midst of the fun and laughter and hang out until others started to leave. As I left, I wondered how I would navigate future family functions. As best I could figure, God would be with me at each event, patiently carrying me until the pain was gone, whispering His love for me in my ear, for however long it would take for the joy to return.

Your Space

THE FIRST "FAMILY" EVENT

You have searched me and known me.
You know my sitting down and my rising up; You understand my thought afar off.
You comprehend my path and my lying down, And are acquainted with all my ways.
For there is not a word on my tongue, But behold, O LORD, You know it altogether.
You have hedged me behind and before, And laid Your hand upon me.
Such knowledge is too wonderful for me; It is high, I cannot attain it.
Where can I go from Your Spirit? Or where can I flee from Your presence?
If I ascend into heaven, You are there; If I make my bed in hell, behold, You are there.
If I take the wings of the morning, And dwell in the uttermost parts of the sea,
Even there Your hand shall lead me, And Your right hand shall hold me.
If I say, "Surely the darkness shall fall on me," Even the night shall be light about me;
Indeed, the darkness shall not hide from You, But the night shines as the day;
The darkness and the light are both alike to You.
For You formed my inward parts; You covered me in my mother's womb.
I will praise You, for I am fearfully and wonderfully made; Marvelous are Your works,
And that my soul knows very well. My frame was not hidden from You,
When I was made in secret, And skillfully wrought in the lowest parts of the earth.
Your eyes saw my substance, being yet unformed. And in Your book they all were written,
The days fashioned for me, When as yet there were none of them.
How precious also are Your thoughts to me, O God!

Psalms 139:1-17

What was your first family gathering after the divorce? How did you manage to get through the event?

_____
_____
_____
_____

Is your family making it easier or harder for you to heal? How?

_____
_____
_____
_____

The Magnet

I've been living alone now for about fourteen weeks. In this time God has done some profound things, including taking the life that I used to know and slowing it down. It once felt like a plummeting plane, crashing to the Earth, but He has slowed it to a glider-like pace and steered me away from making impulsive, self-destructive decisions.

While I have spent these past three months seeking God's purpose for me, He has put very specific people in my path. It's like I've become a magnet for men and women (though mostly the latter) whose lives have been changed by divorce. These people are either experiencing or have experienced rocky marriages or divorce. Various catalysts have caused their relationship problems, and while some are in deep pain, others are finding their way through the many stages of healing.

Although I don't feel particularly qualified to comment on anything but my own broken marriage, the Lord has surrounded me with individuals who need my support. Somehow, in my own personal state of seeming uselessness, God has found a place for me, one in which I can love and lift up those who are suffering relationship neglect or abandonment and let them know that they are not alone.

I have learned to be a better listener, and my limping spirit can't help but want to step up and nurture those who are suffering from their own traumas and feelings of hopelessness. Even though I feel like a puddle of yesterday's spilled milk upon the floor, the Lord has given me focus for what remains so dear to Him–loving others and reaching out to those in need. Though I felt like I had nothing left to give God, He has provided sustenance for my soul and given purpose and direction to my steps. I pray that He will guide the paths of the hurting the way He has guided mine.

Thank you, God, for finding usefulness in me, even when I am exhausted, alone, and so very sad. You can truly draw something from nothing and make it spectacular for Your kingdom. I am weak, but You are strong.

Your Space

Your Space

THE MAGNET

"Let brotherly love continue. Do not forget to entertain strangers, for by so doing some have unwittingly entertained angels."

Hebrews 13:1-2

*"And He said to them, **'It is not for you to know times or seasons which the Father has put in His own authority. But you shall receive power when the Holy Spirit has come upon you; and you shall be witnesses to Me in Jerusalem, and in all Judea and Samaria, and to the end of the earth.'**"*

Acts 1:7-8

Have you discovered a sense of purpose, even with divorce taking up so much time and energy in your life? What is it?

_____
_____
_____
_____

How has this purpose helped you? Has it changed your perspective regarding your personal situation?

_____
_____
_____
_____

The Nightly Routine

I find that I am on my knees at my bedside constantly now. Sometimes, I just kneel quietly and listen, but mostly I talk to God about when my anguish will pass.

"God, I just hurt. Please make it stop. Could you please return to take me home so that my suffering will finally end? I don't know how I am supposed to cope. I feel so alone."

Often, I weep, my shoulders and heart heavy with grief. I spend much more time with the Lord than the once-typical two or three minute bedtime prayer. When he left, I felt like I was completely and utterly exposed to my Maker in every way. I had always known that He saw everything with me and in me, but now His awesome presence seemed to envelope me to the very depths of my soul. Feeling like I was a naked infant once again, I craved comfort and asked Him repeatedly to wrap His arms around me and hold me until the healing was done.

Many evenings, my dreams were horrific and gave me panic attacks, which in turn deprived me of the little sleep I succeeded in almost getting. I remember a night about two months after he walked out, when I felt like a shapeless and energy-less mass, simply existing and aching with loneliness, a lifeless body lying in the dark and staring at the ceiling and walls. I prayed to Jesus for comfort, that He would come and be my companion through this emotional and physical famine of divorce. That very night, I had a vivid dream....

I am getting off of a plane. I am standing at the top of the stairs, looking out on the tarmac at the surrounding mountains and coast. I realize that I have finally made it to Hawaii (having wanted to go my entire life)! As I descend the stairs, I notice that the colors aren't as dramatic in person, like there is a film over the landscape, giving everything a dull appearance. I flash forward to talking with my dad in the hotel lobby. He is off to play golf and asks if I would like to join him. I tell him that I'd rather go see the sights and take off in a rental car. Everywhere I go, the scenery disappoints me. All of the pictures I'd seen and stories I'd heard didn't compare to the actual trip.

I end up finding a relatively secluded piece of beach and park there. I decide to go for a swim to try and wash away this major let-down. For some reason, there are no waves on the beach, so I paddle out into the ocean without a fight. As I step into the surf, I spot a small, wooden float about three hundred yards from shore. It is like the ones you see on a lake, where people can climb out, sunbathe, and dive off. I close the distance in no time at all, even though I am swimming very leisurely. I notice that the water's muted color slips away as I get farther out. Then I am surrounded by such a magnificent blue that it almost radiates, like the hues of a sunset that stir your heart. No one is on the float, so I climb onto it and look around.

The land has vanished, and the sky has become its own bright blue jewel contrasting with the amazing water. I am initially shocked by the fact that I can no longer see Hawaii, but at some level I calmly accept it and simply bask in the brilliance of water and sky. As I turn back to my original position at the top of the ladder, there is a man standing on the float with me. He is taller than I and very tan. He's wearing extra-long bright yellow swim trunks and appears to be someone Hawaiian. I am struck by how beautiful he is; I never refer to men as beautiful... but he is. He smiles, walks to one side of the float, and stretches out on the deck. With one arm tucked back behind his head, he looks up at me and uses his other hand to beckon me over to join him. He never speaks a word. I walk over, stretch out next to him, and sidle up against him. I remember tucking my face up against his side with my cheek on his chest as he gently takes his arm and wraps it around me. I close my eyes and slip into such a peaceful state... the warmth of his body against my cheek, the subtle rocking of the float, the sunlight's comforting presence on my skin, the lapping of water against the side–the only sound in my ears, and the touch of his arm against my back; these are the only sensations in my world.

I have no thoughts or worries of my missing loved ones, or my disappointment with Hawaii, or concerns about work back at the office. I am perfectly content being with this man for as long as I can in this place. He provides me with everything that seems to be lacking in my life and asks nothing in return. He ministers to me in a way I have never before experienced. It ends far too soon, when my alarm clock cries out. However, when I wake, I feel so blessed that God has answered my prayer and brought me peace, even if it feels like it had only been for a moment in time.

Thank you, Lord, for such a quick answer and reminder that I am never alone.

Your Space

THE NIGHTLY ROUTINE

*"Then He said to His disciples, '**Therefore I say to you, do not worry about your life, what you will eat; nor about the body, what you will put on. Life is more than food, and the body is more than clothing. Consider the ravens, for they neither sow nor reap, which have neither storehouse nor barn; and God feeds them. Of how much more value are you than the birds? And which of you by worrying can add one cubit to his stature? If you then are not able to do the least, why are you anxious for the rest? Consider the lilies, how they grow: they neither toil nor spin; and yet I say to you, even Solomon in all his glory was not arrayed like one of these. If then God so clothes the grass, which today is in the field and tomorrow is thrown into the oven, how much more will He clothe you, O you of little faith? And do not seek what you should eat or what you should drink, nor have an anxious mind. For all these things the nations of the world seek after, and your Father knows that you need these things. But seek the kingdom of God, and all these things shall be added to you. Do not fear, little flock, for it is your Father's good pleasure to give you the kingdom.'"*

Luke 12:22-32

Have you found comfort during your divorce? Who or what brought you that comfort?

_____
_____
_____
_____

Have you asked the Lord for anything to help you get through the long days and nights? If so, what? Has He answered your prayer yet? How?

_____
_____
_____
_____

Clarity

After giving my husband space for the last four months (since his walking out and getting an apartment), I received an email from him last Monday stating that he was considering filing an uncontested divorce. The note sabotaged me at work, but I pulled myself together, tried to respond with love, kindness, and patience, then actually had to 'deal' with it at lunch and later that evening. After a couple of meltdowns and flashes of anger and disbelief, I had a sudden and clear revelation. Our marriage was over.

It's like God showed me that I needed to agree to the divorce because He has plans for me. He had allowed me to exhaust every option for healing, forgiveness, counseling, and prayer before letting me know that I had done everything I could to reach him. On the flip side, He also showed me that he had not made any obvious effort to work on our situation via the several possibilities we had discussed, all of which still left me abandoned with no reasonable expectation of growth or movement on his part.

So the rings that never came off, except when I used to cut his hair or make him meatloaf from scratch, were taken off (what are broken promises worth anyway?) and put in a safe place, and for the first time I made an active effort to separate myself from my husband. I had spent so many months praying and talking to God about believing in His miracles and mercy. Although I still trusted in the existence of those things, I also realized at this point that the answer might be "No," and I didn't want to continue to bang my forehead against the proverbial wall.

I began to distance myself in every way I could. I sat down and created an outline of our assets and debts. I rewrote my will and revised my Advanced Medical Directive. On Tuesday I changed all of the beneficiaries on the policies and accounts I had at work and then went to the banks to do the same the following day. I collected all of my important legal documents that would need updating. I started calling a few close friends and asked if they had a reference for a Christian divorce attorney to help me through a settlement agreement. I began brainstorming and making a list of family and friends I could possibly stay with, when needed, during the process. I took his phone numbers and those of his friends out of my cell phone. I made a list of people I could call to help me move when the time came. I didn't desire a divorce, but I seemed to be the only person in the relationship hoping for a resolution that involved us staying married. I did not believe in divorce, but unfortunately my spouse did.

All I knew was that the Lord had never left me, and that week He showered me with His grace and peace. I was calm and mourned the loss of my marriage, but I also celebrated the promise of hope and happiness that God had made me.

I am thankful for the comfort He has given me in dreams, my workplace, my home, through family and friends, and through prayer. I honor Him for all that He has provided in my inability to do for myself. I accept that He has much for me to do, and He wants me to be healthy and equipped to pursue His work. I am not here to struggle and beg for attention and love from anyone. I am already loved by my Creator, and He will bring me the desires of my heart–in love, companionship, family, and most importantly, ministry.

Thank you, Jesus, for being my husband and filling these vast, empty spaces with Your presence.

Your Space

CLARITY

"And now I say to you, keep away from these men and let them alone: for if this plan or this work is of men, it will come to nothing; but if it is of God, you cannot overthrow it – lest you even be found to fight against God."
Acts 5:38-39

"For if, after they have escaped the pollutions of the world through the knowledge of the LORD and Savior Jesus Christ, they are again entangled in them and overcome, the latter end is worse for them than the beginning. For it would have been better for them not to have known the way of righteousness, than having known it, to turn from the holy commandment delivered to them. But it has happened to them according to the true proverb: 'A dog returns to his own vomit,' and, 'a sow, having washed, to her wallowing in the mire.'"
2 Peter 2:20-22

Has divorce shown you something you didn't see before? What?

_____
_____
_____
_____

How will this knowledge change your outlook? Do you feel like this experience will improve or worsen the quality of your life? Why?

_____
_____
_____
_____

Guilt

Someone once told me that *you* are the only person who can make you feel guilty about anything–whether it is a matter of your own conscience and actions or something that relates to interactions with other people. You either have to willingly accept guilty feelings or deny them. At some point during the last several years, I had permitted guilt to have more and more power in my life. It reached such toxic levels that I actually began to believe that the destruction of my marriage was my fault. Over and over again, I replayed different scenarios in my mind, searching for the moment or situation in which I had failed my husband. I tried to figure out what those shortcomings were in order to prevent myself from repeating them. It was only after he left that I acquired a clearer perspective.

First, I realized that it wasn't solely my responsibility to fix our marriage–that it required God (above all else) and two willing participants. Second, I claimed more accountability than was truly mine to bear. Somehow, I had let myself absorb projected problems that weren't really mine at all, yet I diligently struggled to try and find the solutions for them. Last, I needed to create a protective boundary for myself – one that would buffer me from reacting to other people's actions with guilt. Therefore, I decided not to permit myself any further feelings of guilt about the split. I trusted that, in surrendering my life to God, He would deliver me from my unhealthy emotions which had become distorted by the pain of the divorce. I could not continue to look back and wonder, "What if I'd done this or said that?"

I no longer take responsibility for variables outside my control. I refuse to allow unhealthy guilt to take up any more space in my life.

I have done everything I can, Lord, and I know that You will take care of whatever I am unable to do.

Your Space

Your Space

GUILT

"It is better to trust in the LORD Than to put confidence in man."

Psalms 118:8

"And God is able to make all grace abound toward you, that you, always having all sufficiency in all things, may have abundance for every good work."

2 Corinthians 9:8

What role did guilt play in your divorce?

_____
_____
_____
_____

If you feel guilty, do you believe that those feelings will change with time? Why or why not?

_____
_____
_____
_____

Back from "We" to "I"

The shift from "I" into "we" felt so natural. I embraced it excitedly, as the words were an indication of the sweet, growing bond between us–a friendship, love, and companionship that was unlike any I'd ever had with a man. It held the promise of hopes, dreams, and adventures, all tied together with devotion, hard work, and (of course) God's love. We courted for five and a half years and were married for almost eleven when he decided that we were no more. Until that moment, I didn't know what people meant when they talked about being trapped in a relationship.

The word "trapped" implied that one person had all of the control and the other person none. Suddenly, I had no power, and my life was forced onto a course that I didn't want. He made it clear that, not only was our partnership over, but our friendship was over as well. Everything I had been doing for him or for us now became a matter of basic survival for me. I began to learn how to ask for help from family, friends, coworkers, and neighbors, because I was not equipped to care for "our" home, animals, and responsibilities as an individual. I grimaced any time I had to fill out a form and mark my marital status. I was irritated at having to take time off of work to coordinate with deliveries or repair people whom he normally would have handled in the past. I was embarrassed by having to ask people to drive me out of town for my many sessions of back treatments (that I needed badly and assumed he would have been around to support). In addition, I had no one around anymore to care for me when I got sick, including the week he left when I came down with bronchitis. The reality of the "I" caught in a loveless marriage was agonizing.

My therapist was encouraging, but she emphasized that each person processed trauma and healed at different rates; there usually were no quick fixes. This state was impossible to explain to my heart. How could I tell it that seventeen years of love, growth, and warmth had now been rendered void? The "we" had left, and only the pain of vacancy remained. My brain fully grasped that the "I" had returned, but my heart continued to repeatedly slip and include a "we" here and there in conversation.

God, when will this be finished? What are you going to do with all of that "we" time that has been thrown away? Would you please help me find the "I" that is pleasing to you and help her start over? Would you be my "we"?

Your Space

BACK FROM "WE" TO "I"

"I will instruct you and teach you in the way you should go; I will guide you with My eye."
                                                                    Psalms 32:8

What difficulties did you have in going from being married to being single again?
_____
_____
_____
_____

Was it a relief or a burden? Did you uncover more relationship issues during the transition?
_____
_____
_____
_____

My Everything

In my opinion, the old adage that "You don't know what you've got until it's gone" could be easily changed to "You don't know what God truly means to you until the distractions in your life are gone."

The Lord has been my friend and confidant my entire life. I have prayed in thanksgiving and spoken to Him every day. But, it wasn't until my husband left that I got an amazing taste of the Lord's mercy and love. I knew He was always there, I believed in and expected miracles, and I'd even heard His voice speak to me on two occasions. However, that was small stuff compared to how He has become my everything. Specifically, I'd like to address two areas where He has provided for me in different ways: money and sex/intimacy.

First, I had no idea how I would be able to pay the bills, especially since "we" had been living off of my income and an equity line for three years. With the equity line gone, fear and panic crept up on me at random times, even before the divorce was final.

So I found myself before my true and faithful holy Husband and Father, asking Him to lift the burden from my shoulders, because no matter how many tutorials or odd jobs I got, I couldn't make the money I needed to support myself and the house, that had suddenly become solely my responsibility. And He did–not in a winning-lottery-ticket sort of way, but in a quiet, glorious series of events sewn together as a warm blanket just for me.

He blessed me with offerings of cash and gift cards from family members, friends, and strangers. He sent me refund checks for overpayments I don't remember making. He treated me to meals out at others' homes and as their guest at local restaurants. He gave me opportunities to use payment plans and "same-as-cash" financing for much-needed home improvements and to pay medical bills. He generated additional income once I was able to cancel and change policies that related to my husband. Whenever I needed extra funds for a bill, He brought me an opportunity for extra work. He provided enough of a tax refund to cover my hefty property taxes. The list goes on and on, but you get the idea. I can't explain it, nor do I have to. Grace is what it is. Besides, I don't need to know the how when I already know the why: His Word says He will provide for widows, and I have asked Him to do just that.

At first, addressing the second topic of physical intimacy, was devastating. I would wither up and die without physical contact, and I wasn't sure how much longer I could bear living in complete isolation. I had been praying for a miracle healing of our marriage, but when I realized nothing was changing on my husband's end, I began to ask for God's comfort. I'd always known that He could do anything, and so I humbly and anxiously asked Him to turn my flesh "off." I prayed for Him to get me through whatever period of time I could handle without fixating on the absence of a physical relationship. And He did.

Within a few days, He had removed the desire to be touched from my heart. My brain couldn't believe what was happening, as that whole part of my being that longed for a physical relationship seemed distant. Yet, my spirit rejoiced in having the pain relieved. I don't know why I was so shocked when it actually happened. After all, He had created those feelings and given them to me, so He could obviously take them away.

In addition to the issues which He handled for me, His Holy Spirit also came and stayed with me whenever I needed Him. He kept me from utter desperation. At night He made me feel safe. I felt loved and protected by my unseen companion. He gradually replaced heartache with glimpses of healing and touches of joy and laughter again. His constant presence reminded me of the power of hope.

There are not enough words or pages to describe how grateful I am for Him. He is my everything, and I have never known a love like I do for the Lord. Everyone and everything else represents added blessings poured out on my life by my one true love.

Thank you, Lord, for being ever-faithful and fulfilling all of your promises.

Your Space

MY EVERYTHING

"I sought the LORD, and He heard me, And delivered me from all my fears... "
Psalms 34:4

"If you abide in Me, and My words abide in you, you will ask what you desire, and it shall be done for you."
John 15:7

In the scheme of your life, what part does God play? Does He have a central role, or is it more of an occasional one?

_____
_____
_____
_____

Have the circumstances of your divorce brought you closer to or moved you further from Him? Why?

_____
_____
_____
_____

Mutual Friends

With my world still upside down, I had to confront another aspect of the divorce–our mutual friends and acquaintances, some of whom knew of our situation. This put me in a very awkward position when I received phone calls and invitations, bumped into people in public, or attended social events alone. Usually, the exchange would be short and to the point.

"Well, he left me back in May, so now I'm trying to figure out what the Lord would like me to do with the rest of my life." Talk about a conversation killer!

Everyone was shocked, and most wanted some explanation as to the why, when, how–something that would help them get a rational grasp on our situation. But I had nothing to offer them, since it was hard enough to get through the exchanges without bursting into tears. I had no reassurance to give them, especially not to those who had known us since we first met. The truest of friends stayed in touch with both of us. Our individual friends also gave whatever support they could. However, there were some sweet and kind people with whom I could no longer associate due to their business and personal relationships with him.

I mourned the loss of this adopted family who had taken me in a decade ago, as well as others who I knew would probably drift away over time. I'd never had people cut out of my life unless I had chosen to sever the relationship. Losing them in this way was a frustrating experience. Now there was this weird, unspoken strangeness when I would talk to or hang out with our mutual friends, like a deep pain that suddenly hung over every conversation or get-together, something that hurt but could not easily be discussed or healed, more than one heart grief-stricken by a love that was gone. They hurt for me, for him, and for themselves. And I am helpless, with nothing to say or do for them or myself to resolve the pain and suffering, for only God can mend the soul.

Lord, please mend mine.

Your Space

Your Space

MUTUAL FRIENDS

"Let your speech always be with grace, seasoned with salt, that you may know how you ought to answer... "

Colossians 4:6

How has your relationship with mutual friends been affected by your divorce?

_____
_____
_____
_____

Have you taken steps to emotionally protect yourself? What are they? How do you answer those awkward questions about your ex-spouse?

_____
_____
_____
_____

⚜

"Not Yet" Is the Answer

For the last five or six years, I have been on my knees before the Lord asking Him for children. I took all of the steps I could to track my "progress" each month and even spiffed up my intimate apparel wardrobe to add to the fun. I waited up on nights when I wasn't sure what time he would be home, hoping to spend some quality time together and definitely not minding if it would lead to other things. I dreamed of being pregnant, nursing, and taking care of our infants and toddlers. I could almost smell them when I awoke in the morning.

"Lord, please bless us with the children we desire, so that my husband and I can bring them up to know and love You. Please give us as many as You like, and I ask you to protect them and bring them into this world healthy and strong." I had spoken to Him in prayer, so many times, with the belief that He would bring them in His perfect timing. *Trust Him*, I reminded myself repeatedly.

However, our family never came. I have cried many tears over the children that never were, but now that he has left me, I see how wise and generous God was in protecting me from becoming a single mom. If there is one thing I have heard from many parents, it is that having children never solves anything. Therefore, had the Lord blessed me with what I craved, I would have found myself left all alone, with children to care for as well. And so, my Father sat with me through each round of praying for babies and gently whispered, "Not yet."

Even through the pain of divorce, my heart still yearns for a family. I have asked the Lord to remove this desire from my being, if it is not going to happen. Yet, the feelings remain, and I enthusiastically anticipate the man after God's own heart who will come into my life and create a family that loves the Lord with me.

Thank you, God, for keeping me safe from the disaster that could have been, had you granted me the desires of my heart during years past. I trust you and your amazing love through all things–especially when the answer is "No."

Your Space

"NOT YET" IS THE ANSWER

(Hannah's prayer in thanks for having a son after being barren)

"My heart rejoices in the LORD;
My horn is exalted in the LORD. I smile at my enemies,
Because I rejoice in Your salvation.

No one is holy like the LORD, For there is none besides You,
Nor is there any rock like our God.

Talk no more so very proudly; Let no arrogance come from your mouth,
For the LORD is the God of knowledge; And by Him actions are weighed.

The bows of the mighty men are broken, And those who stumbled are girded with strength. Those who were full have hired themselves out for bread, And the hungry have ceased to hunger. Even the barren has borne seven, And she who has many children has become feeble.

The LORD kills and makes alive; He brings down to the grave and brings up.
The LORD makes poor and makes rich; He brings low and lifts up.
He raises the poor from the dust And lifts the beggar from the ash heap,
To set them among princes And make them inherit the throne of glory.

For the pillars of the earth are the LORD's, And He has set the world upon them.
He will guard the feet of His saints, But the wicked shall be silent in darkness.
For by strength no man shall prevail.

The adversaries of the LORD shall be broken in pieces;
From heaven He will thunder against them.
The LORD will judge the ends of the earth.
He will give strength to His king, And exalt the horn of His anointed."

1 Samuel 2:1-10

Did you have dreams or desires that went unfulfilled in your marriage?

_____
_____
_____
_____

Have you given up completely on them, or do you still hope to experience them as you embrace the rest of life?

_____
_____
_____
_____

Sweet Ana

As if my heart could even take another blow, we had to put our sweet Ana down yesterday, four months into our separation. She had bone cancer in her front leg, and he called me from the vet to tell me I should come and say goodbye." I didn't know how I could let her go. Ana and our other dog Yoshi were all I had left for companionship, comfort, and love in our home. She had listened to my pain and licked my tears, supporting me in her own special way. Her little nub and "wiggle bottom," as we used to call it, greeted me every time I came into the room, and her cute facial expressions and antics kept me smiling. How would I survive without this gentle presence and without my husband to tell me that everything would be okay? The tears were already streaming down my cheeks when I arrived at the vet.

Ana was her spunky self on the exam room floor, her nub wagging as I stepped through the door. And there he was... the only person I would want to be there with me in this moment: the man who brought our sweet Ana home that first day, who prayed with me during her emergency surgery years later, who built a ramp to make walking easier for her, who snuggled with us on lazy Saturday mornings back when she could still jump onto our bed, and who still came by to help put her outside since I couldn't lift her by myself.

I stretched out only inches from this man I loved, wanting to wake up from this nightmare, find him asleep in the bed next to me, and calm my heart from the panic that had ensued. I wanted to wrap myself up in his arms and hear a few kind words. I wanted to take away his pain and agony from losing her and tell him something comforting. But no words came, and I lay there next to Ana with what was left of my heart dying ever so slowly as the moments ticked by. After an hour an a half passed by, feeling like only a few short minutes, we held our sweet girl and gave her back to God. I ached for the world to stop kicking me and give me time to regroup. I don't remember much of what happened after that except being back home and collecting all of the dog supplies to give to him.

We decided that Yoshi should go with him, and this choice, though best for the dog, left me completely alone, having lost a husband and two dogs in less than four months. Once they left, my house would be empty with only my memories and grief to keep me company. My body cried out to be touched, and I finally turned to him and asked, "Could you please give me a hug... just for a second?" Fortunately, he agreed and gave me a moment or two to seek whatever comfort I could draw from the short embrace. I closed my eyes and willed time to stand still, since I didn't know if this would be the last physical contact we might ever have.

Thoughts of the four of us camping, traveling, and just being silly on the living room floor flashed behind my eyes. Then he backed away, turned, and left with our other dog tagging along, oblivious that his buddy was gone forever. For the rest of the day, I was curled up in a ball on the floor seeking escape from this reality.

Where are you, Lord? How much pain can I take before my brain decides it's too much and fails me completely? How will I cope with not having my babies to keep me company, and play, and walk with me in the mornings? How will I go on? Please help me, God. I am a desperately hurting woman who has nothing left inside. Don't let me lose hope... not ever.

Your Space

SWEET ANA

"For where your treasure is, there your heart will also be."

Luke 12:34

During your divorce did you have other, unexpected losses that sank you even deeper into mourning?

_____
_____
_____
_____

How did you cope with those events?

_____
_____
_____
_____

God's Messengers

I don't think that any of us pictures ourselves actively needing help with our lives. We assume that, except for emergencies, our self-sufficiency will see us through. But I've had two major crises in the last three years that opened my eyes to how *in*sufficient I can be on my own. The first was the back injury I suffered in January of 2006. The second was my divorce. Both of these experiences isolated me from my daily routine and taught me to embrace the realization that I can't do it all by myself– and that is okay. I've spent many days and nights in tears from not being able to complete chores, do yard work, whip through simple projects, or move heavy things. But even in my feelings of helplessness, God sent his angels to help me. They've come in droves.

My parents and sister have been present daily with notes, calls, emails, and little gifts, even though they also have a tremendous number of their own challenges this year. My best friend and her parents have seemingly created a fan club of love for me, with their cards and care packages arriving monthly and always bringing me smiles and awe at their attentiveness and generosity. My sweet neighbors have helped me with my yard work for months and months and months, because I am unable to mow my lawn and dump the clippings without pain. Others have brought over food at just the right times, when I felt particularly alone and in need of love. I would find a kind note in my mailbox now and then, and some neighbors would make a point of stopping by on walks to share their dogs with me, knowing that both of mine are gone. If I didn't feel like calling my parents or anyone else long distance, I could walk across the street and sit with another special family and talk, cry, or pray. One night several of the guys from the surrounding houses came by and dragged all of the old appliances out of my kitchen (on a rainy evening, no less) and moved the new ones in because I had to put my house on the market, and I was far from being able to move even one piece by myself. The selflessness of my neighbors has been amazing.

Even though the separation had made celebrating my birthday difficult, many family members and friends (toting flowers, cake, cards, and hugs) came by to honor my special day. At work, my second family would shoot me emails, drop notes on my desk, or leave tokens of love, whether pieces of fruit or something homemade to let me know they were watching over me. When I went in search of a hug, they were always there to let me vent or cry. In addition, I have made numerous monthly visits to my back doctor's office (two hours from my house), and I have never wanted for someone who would give up most of a day to drive me down and back and hold my hand through the actual treatments. Even when people had to cancel at the last minute, another person would suddenly become available.

    I have also had the blessings of material gifts: unexpected checks in the mail, a new garage door opener when mine broke, dishes, books, clothing, and grocery store and gas gift cards. So though I have been physically alone for a very long time, God has sent His amazing children to take care of me. He has provided in all ways what I couldn't do for myself, and then even more, a LOT more.

Your Space

GOD'S MESSENGERS

"But this I say: He who sows sparingly will also reap sparingly, and he who sows bountifully will also reap bountifully. So let each one give as he purposes in his heart, not grudgingly or of necessity; for God loves a cheerful giver."

II Corinthians 9:6-7

Did you have anyone who made an effort to help you when your divorce became known?

_____
_____
_____
_____

In what way did family and friends reach out to you?

_____
_____
_____
_____

Have you ever reached out to someone else who was going through a divorce? How?

_____
_____
_____
_____

Out of Order

Today, my pastor taught about the spiritual presence of God and His power. He emphasized the premise that, as we surrender our spiritual selves to the Lord, He will bless our spiritual obedience by meeting our physical, emotional, and spiritual needs, providing health to our bodies, strength in our relationships, contentment with our careers, financial provision, and many other necessities. As he cross-referenced several Scriptures that reiterated this train of thought, I put my failed marriage into the spiritual equation.

I began to see more and more that it had been out of order with God's instruction. We had lacked mutual surrender and trust in the Lord, so our union floundered. No matter how hard each of us tried to work on our relationship or improve our situation in some way, we failed to salvage our marriage because we had not jointly placed all of it before God to do with as He saw fit. We had done our best to control and force the physical world into a formula we thought would work, but there was little spiritual foundation upon which to build. We gave ourselves too much credit and responsibility when it was the Lord's wisdom and guidance that would have improved every aspect of our lives, had we humbled ourselves together before Him. I also realized that neither of us could be a substitute for the other, no matter how hard either of us tried. No one can step in and cover for another. The Lord wanted each of us to give Him his full attention and commitment, and we didn't.

I see now why the struggle became harder. We ended up going in opposite directions from each other and therefore from God. We could have been individually and jointly healed, and all of our woes and challenges could have been eagerly conquered by the Lord. But instead, our relationship and everything connected to it died.

Lord Jesus, please rebuild a life for me as You would have it, with joy and happiness that only You can give, with a heart that longs for Your love and guidance, and with the provision that Your wisdom and grace will shower over every minute of my days. I trust in You, and You alone, to bring me the peace and life I desire. Tell me what You would have for my life, order it as You see fit, and I will do my best to fulfill it.

Your Space

Your Space

OUT OF ORDER

"Let no one say when he is tempted, 'I am tempted by God';
for God cannot be tempted by evil, nor does He Himself tempt anyone.
But each one is tempted when he is drawn away by his own desires and enticed."

James 1:13-14

"...But as for me and my house, we will serve the LORD."

Joshua 24.15

What part(s) of your marriage were out of order with God's instructions?

_____
_____
_____
_____

Were these a result of your behavior, your spouse's, or a combination of both?

_____
_____
_____
_____

How will identifying these actions now help you with future relationships?

_____
_____
_____
_____

Snapshots

One of the hardest parts of trying to get through a divorce is the constant presence of pictures. Now, unless you are a professional photo-journalist, pictures evoke mostly positive memories. We flip back (or scroll, nowadays) through dozens of shots that make us smile, laugh, cry, and sometimes blush. Photos are social magnets that invite people to oogle, hear stories, and add anecdotes of their own. All of that fondness and reminiscing changes during a divorce. Suddenly, everywhere I look I see his face, and I hurt. The worst part is that each pain is different, depending on the memory.

When I come across a shot from our early dating years, I feel sad and wonder where the simplistic days–when we savored any glimpses of each other or quality time together–went. I still remember one night at a local miniature golf place. He had won some tickets in the arcade and bought me a surprise. As he walked over, he told me to close my eyes and hold out my hands. When I was able to open my eyes, I found a tiny, hot pink rope ring in my palm. He plucked it back up and put it on my ring finger.

"This is until I can get you something better," he had said with a grin.

The photos of family events make me lonely, since I've attended so many by myself, and they remind me of the family I had envisioned we would have one day. I recall how we laughed so hard during the numerous celebrations we attended over the last seventeen years. My family loves him deeply, and they are mourning for our split as well.

Pictures of our wedding give me heartache, and I wonder how we became so distant from the true happiness and joy we once gave each other. I remember when he turned to me at our first honeymoon dinner and said, "This was the most fun I've ever had at a wedding. I'm glad we did it our way." I had agreed wholeheartedly, elated with such an incredible beginning to our married life together. And now it was over.

When I see a photo of him alone, I wonder if he is okay, if he really knows how much I love him, and if he will ever see himself the way the rest of the world and I see him–as a phenomenal man with a huge heart whom I have cherished for half of my life.

"I love you so much, just the way you are. I don't care where we go or what we do, as long as we do it together. We can get through anything that life throws at us." How many times had I said those very words, believing them to be the truth?

If the shot is of the two of us, it reminds me of his touch and smell that I've missed for what seems like forever. Now, wanting to distance myself from that pain, I have thought about throwing the pictures away.

"I'm not sure if I even want to keep any visual reminders of what used to be," I told a dear friend. "Maybe that will change, but I can't imagine how."

Even though I've tried to remove as many of them as I can from home and work, I still come across them too often. My parents took theirs down as well, but I remember each one's place and content vividly. They jerk at my heartstrings in a way beyond my control.

I hope, Lord, that there will come a day when I can say his name and see his picture and not experience any pain. Please help me find the antidote for this anguish, so I can move on. I cannot take back what I have already given freely in love, and I have loved too deeply to heal this wound on my own. God, please hear me and lighten my heavy burden.

Your Space

SNAPSHOTS

"But the fruit of the Spirit is love, joy, peace, longsuffering, kindness, goodness, faithfulness, gentleness, self-control. Against such there is no law."

Galatians 5:22-23

How have pictures affected you since the divorce process began?

_____
_____
_____
_____

How do you deal with the emotions they evoke?

_____
_____
_____
_____

⚘

Stumbling Block

I'm actually early for tomorrow's breakfast preparations, I thought, glancing at my cell phone. The rain pounded down on my car as I sat waiting for the light to change. My thoughts drifted momentarily to him and the fact that he had been gone for over six months now. In my rear view mirror I saw a red car roll to a stop behind me. I pictured my little Yoshi and pondered how he was doing without Ana. My thoughts turned back to tomorrow's event, wondering how many people would be at the women's breakfast. My eyes drifted back to my phone. Fifteen minutes and only three blocks to go.

The next moment brought shock and disbelief, as a large truck approaching from behind the red car failed to stop and slammed into it, which in turn slammed into me. There was no screeching of tires on the wet road or even the sound of the primary impact, only the explosion of pain in my head and neck. In the period of a split second, my life changed yet again, with another crisis to remind me of my husband's absence and my own vulnerability.

As I rode in the ambulance strapped to the stretcher board, brace around my head and neck, back hurting, with thoughts of *I hope my car will be okay,* I answered the paramedic's questions. Age? Blah. Address? Blah blah blah. Married? Yes (*What a joke,* my heart remarked). I couldn't even call him for fear of getting a "Not interested" or "Don't care" response. So I called my cousin and another friend instead.

My couple of hours alone in the ER gave me time to talk to the Lord and thank Him for His ongoing faithfulness, the quick response time from the police and ambulance, my medical insurance, and the love of people to care for me. His presence was a true consolation as I struggled to tolerate being strapped down (the position worsened my pre-existing back injury). I knew my frustration and doubts would subside with time, and I reflected on how often the Scripture instructs us to be patient with matters of the Lord.

So I took my faith and kicked the accident stumbling block back out into the hospital corridor. I embraced my circumstances and vowed to remember them, because I knew that God would use them to do something good... I just wasn't sure exactly how or when it would happen.

Well, God, You didn't cause my accident, but You continue to have my full attention and desire for service, even as the minutes drag by. Please show me what I can do to fulfill Your purposes through these less-than-favorable circumstances. Thank you for staying with me, seeing me through another painful experience, and always catching me when I stumble.

Your Space

STUMBLING BLOCK

"Rejoice always, pray without ceasing, in everything give thanks; for this is the will of God in Christ Jesus for you."

1 Thessalonians 5:16-18

What hurdles has the enemy thrown in front of you since your divorce process began? What strategies helped you to cope with them?

_____
_____
_____
_____

Have these hurdles encouraged you to reach out to for support in ways different than you were used to? How so?

_____
_____
_____
_____

The Different Thanksgiving

The train ride would have made the visit feel like a simple trip up to see Mom and Dad, but his absence engulfed me and thwarted all attempts I made to create a feeling of normalcy for this Thanksgiving. I spent last year's celebration alone for several days, as he had planned "work" during what would normally have been travel/family time, leaving me only with the company of my dogs. This holiday would be the first time I'd been together with my mom, dad, and sister since he had left.

Holding my grief at bay during the most regular of activities was an enormous challenge. I didn't have anything I really wanted or needed to talk about, but I didn't want to be the party killer either. Whenever I could, I tucked myself away to cry, especially at night as I gazed at the empty space in the bed next to me and the sign on the wall that read "Granddoggies Spoiled Here." I ached for the companionship of even one of my dogs, but Ana had been put down only three months ago, and Yoshi was no longer part of my family.

The days felt extremely slow and long. The minutes that should have provided rest and relaxation only strained my patience and grief. I wanted to share with my family, but I didn't want to become the center of attention and dwell even more on my painful circumstances. Most of Mom and Dad's support of me was nonverbal, but occasionally one of them would offer "Are you okay?" For the first time in my life, my adopted response became "No, but I will be." I managed, with their help, to get through the time with some moments of peace and laughter. In addition, my parents' golden retriever spent a lot of time with his head in my lap or lying at my feet and sleeping with me on my bed, knowing that my heart was hurting and doing his best to give me what support he could.

During the Thanksgiving meal I did all I could not to let my tears fall, especially during the blessing. I thought about where he could be and hoped that he had someone with whom he could spend such a special time. I pictured him together with my sweet Yoshi, sitting and watching football.

I asked the Lord to provide him with whatever he needed to get through the holidays, because I knew that he must be hurting too, only in a different way. I silently mourned the fact that I didn't have the cure for his pain. I also grieved the fact that I still loved him.

Your Space

THE DIFFERENT THANKSGIVING

"Is there anything too hard for the LORD?"

Genesis 18:14

How would you describe the first holiday celebration that occurred in the middle of your divorce?

_____
_____
_____
_____

What times pained you the most deeply? Why?

_____
_____
_____
_____

How were you able to cope with those pains?

_____
_____
_____
_____

Giving Up the Crate

Last night, I received a call from one of my neighbors down the street.

"Hi, Melanie. We just adopted a five-month-old Boxer, and I was wondering if you still had an extra kennel that we could buy from you? I know you had planned to sell it in a yard sale, but would you mind if we got it first?"

My mind shifted to the crate, sitting in the corner of the garage, still holding a piece of carpet in its tray. I told her she was welcome to have it (since I am unable to have a dog right now). I paused the movie I had rented and headed downstairs to the basement with a few rags in hand to clean the crate. I had managed to put the memory of my dogs' faces, kisses, and cuteness at arm's length during the divorce process. I had tried my best to ignore the profound emptiness in my home and the constant loneliness I felt for their company. But as I dragged the crate from its niche of protection (covered with ceiling tiles and wedged between chairs and tables), the memories of Ana and Yoshi flooded to the forefront of my mind.

As I began to wipe off the dust and dog hair, my tears flowed. I saw both of my babies back when we first adopted them–Ana with her nervous shaking, chattering teeth, and unsure glances, and Yoshi's three-month-old body that had some catching up to do with his big ears and paws. I couldn't hold my pain in any longer, so I clung to the crate and sobbed, letting out deep, guttural moans–sounds that only come from unconditional love lost. Many minutes passed as my heart released its storehouses of grief, but I knew that giving up the crate was another step in God's new beginning for my life.

One day, when I am in a new place, I will welcome new dogs and new memories into my being. But for now, I need to process and release certain feelings, or else I will never be able to fully heal from losing so much at one time. I am blessed to have the Lord carrying me through it at a pace He knows I can handle. He is an awesome God and wants me to be free of my pain and embrace the happiness He has waiting for me. I celebrate the anticipation of its arrival.

I pray, Lord, that you will help me to continue healing and leave these pieces of personal devastation behind me. I want to soak in the unconditional love of dogs in my family again one day. Please make it soon.

Your Space

GIVING UP THE CRATE

"Now faith is the substance of things hoped for, the evidence of things not seen."
Hebrews 11:1

Did you have to make unexpected sacrifices during your divorce? What were they?
___
___
___
___

Did they seem overwhelming to you? What did you do in order to persevere?
___
___
___
___

The "In Between" Christmas

As my divorce's becoming official approaches, I struggled through another "in between" holiday. "In between" was the only way to describe my state, both legal and emotional, during Christmas this year. I was not really married but not really divorced, either. I would say that this state was a version of hell. Though surrounded by loved ones over the holiday weekend, my mind was elsewhere, as the holiday season has brought me lots of time to question my future.

Who am I supposed to picture sitting next to me at mealtimes? In my car? Who will hold me when things aren't going well in my world? Who will dance with me at weddings or under the stars? Who will tell me that I am loved and important? Who will encourage me through the tough spots? Who will care for me when I'm sick? Who will truly desire to have a family with me? Who will be that person now? Will there ever be anyone else?

I managed to get through Christmas to return home to a house mostly devoid of his things. He moved the majority of his belongings while I was gone. Their absence brought a mixture of shock, sadness, and relief. He came back by the house before the weekend was over, but he showed no interest, remorse, affection, or concern for me–an emotional space between us just as empty as the one created by his packing and moving.

I had not given up hope of a miracle, but it appeared that the answer was still "No." What little of an exchange that drifted between us made it clear that he had no more sense of loyalty or commitment towards me–yet another reality check for my heart. The finality of it hung in the air, and I realized that I had to let him go. I could almost hear the Lord gently telling me that I was going to be okay, even with the remnants of carnage left by our relationship scattered all around me. And so he left, and I knew that the promises of love and devotion I'd made to him so many years ago meant nothing to him now.

"I will always love you," I told the closed front door. "Goodbye."

As I watched him drive away, I decided that I was ready to be free of the burden of rejection and abandonment that had laid upon my shoulders for the last several years. I was ready to be loved, accepted, and cherished by a man who is waiting for me as I have been waiting for him. My heart was ready to find a new home.

Your Space

THE "IN BETWEEN" CHRISTMAS

"Therefore, if anyone is in Christ, he is a new creation; old things have passed away; behold, all things have become new."

2 Corinthians 5:17

"And God will wipe away every tear from their eyes; there shall be no more death, nor sorrow, nor crying. There shall be no more pain, for the former things have passed away."

Revelation 21:4

Did you eventually reach a point where you knew in your heart that your marriage was over? When was it? How did you know?

_____
_____
_____
_____

What feelings accompanied that realization? Were you anxious? Relieved? Devastated?

_____
_____
_____
_____

Slamming Doors

I remember my most vivid experiences with slamming doors from childhood. I can hear the sharp and powerful sound of wood-on-wood contact and the consequent reverberation through the house. I recall the heightened emotions (whether mine or someone else's) that would trigger the event. Slamming doors have such a finality to them... like someone screaming "So, there!" or "I'm done talking about it!" or "Go away!" and shutting the world out by sealing that portal to the place where he or she would rather be. We slam doors to get away from what we don't want and ponder what we think we need. Children slam doors on parents who discipline them or refuse to indulge their every whim. Adults do it when arguments become too heated or offenses are too great to deal with at the moment. These partitions are barriers that assist us in processing our decisions and planning our next step in a relationship.

The one slamming the door establishes control and boundaries. The person shut out has to make a choice; will he or she make an effort to redirect the opinion of the angry party? Sometimes, both parties can reach a compromise. Other times, no forward movement is possible, but the person shut out will still stand at the door knocking incessantly and trying to force it open. Generally speaking, slamming doors has come to be viewed as negative, usually because it represents the fact that things aren't going our way.

When considering our spiritual lives, we also use phrases about God closing doors. Unfortunately, we often fail to find the blessing in such a holy gesture. Our perspective usually comes from the angle of "I was really counting on that job," or "Shouldn't it be my turn already?" or "Why can't I get a break?" We are disappointed and frustrated, so we return to the door that was abruptly shut and try to pry it ajar. We pound on it harder and harder, convinced that if we just work more diligently, pray more often, or increase our personal sacrifices, we will open it up again. We do this because we arrogantly project our needs to the other side of the door and set a bee-line for them. However, what lies on the other side is never the truth as we perceive it. The real truth (whether good or bad) is known only to the Lord. What lies behind the door could be tragic. It could devastate, injure, or defeat us completely. All that our minds have to compare that unseen place to is our own set of past expectations and life experiences, limited as they are. We are conditioned to believe we can find a quick fix for our situation or needs behind that one door that has 1) our perfect mate 2) the dream home 3) the ultimate job or 4) fill in your own blank.

Yet, the answer is not behind any single door. It comes from trusting God's incredible wisdom and love to guide you through your own life's collection of doors and not stopping to pry open the doors He closes. The most difficult part of dealing with trust is knowing that you may never understand the reasoning behind the Lord's decisions but having a thankful heart anyway. If challenging paths are open to you, He is right at your side. Just keep moving. There are far worse things than not getting your way, and we have Christ to thank for sparing us from ever having to go through those experiences.

Dear Lord, as tremendous a blow as this divorce has been to my life, I will not try to force the door back open. I gave my marriage everything I had, and I know that You made the best of my efforts. I will keep moving, searching, and listening for Your guidance. Thank you for keeping me from going through doors that would have made the situation even worse. I trust Your choices for my life, so please help me to see them clearly and move into them with confidence.

Your Space

SLAMMING DOORS

"Do not love the world or the things in the world. If anyone loves the world, the love of the Father is not in him."

1 John 2:15

What slamming (or closed) doors have you run into lately? How did you respond to them?

_____
_____
_____
_____

Do you look back on them as positive or negative experiences? Do you see God's presence or absence in them? Explain.

_____
_____
_____
_____

Life without a Rear View Mirror

On my way home from church today, I contemplated what the Lord has in store for me in the new year. Surrounded by shattered dreams, I spent most of last year mourning the loss of my marriage and wondering how I would survive the trauma caused by my husband's departure. All that I had hoped and imagined for my future had been wiped clean. All of the building that I felt had taken place was razed to the ground. My only constant was God's presence in my life and the love and support of family and friends.

But with the upcoming turn from December to January, I realized that I needed to redirect my energy to what lay ahead–for me and the Lord, specifically. I had burned so many hours looking back at my past, saying things like "what if" and praying for a miracle, that it was affecting my ability to move forward and actively seek out what the Lord would have me do with my life. I had become distracted by my own rear view mirror. I began to ask myself, "What is it that you see back there that is so fascinating or helpful?"

Instead of an occasional glance to remind me of how to avoid repeating mistakes and redirecting my steps around problems already dodged, my rear view mirror had become the focus–my past demanding my full attention and thereby stalling my ability to progress into my future in a healthy fashion. So today I pledged to remember the lessons of my personal history but not to spend any more time straining to look back over my shoulder, reliving whatever it was I left back there.

God needs me paying attention in the here and now, and He has already dismissed and forgiven the trail of errors from my days gone by. It is time for me to step up with all of my resources, mind, heart, and spirit for His service. He will call, and I will answer, and I can be certain that His voice will help me find my way to the purposes He has for my life. I no longer need my rear view mirror and its baggage, since all I require from the past is already tucked safely away, for easy reference, in my heart.

Speak loudly and clearly, Lord, and let there be no hesitation in my steps toward Your will.

Your Space

Your Space

LIFE WITHOUT A REARVIEW MIRROR

"I will love You, O LORD, my strength. The LORD is my rock and my fortress and my deliverer; My God my strength in whom I will trust; My shield and the horn of my salvation, my stronghold. I will call upon the LORD, who is worthy to be praised; So shall I be saved from my enemies."

Psalms 18 1:-3

Do you have something distracting you in your own rear view mirror? What is it? Is there more than one thing there holding your attention?

_____
_____
_____
_____

How could your time and attention be better used?

_____
_____
_____
_____

Fear-free

Tonight, I find myself in a marvelous place. The most glorious part of this state of being is the complete absence of fear. Though my husband and I are only weeks from divorce, my house is still for sale, my sinus infection persists, my monthly back treatment was canceled, and I'm worried that the economy may shut down my office due to the selling slump, I rest comfortably on my sofa knowing that God is in control. The old triggers, or things that normally would have me losing sleep, experiencing stomach pain, or suffering from tension headaches, are nowhere to be found. The Lord has put them away and provided me with tranquility. The best thing about it is that I'm not asleep, which is usually one of the only times I can be fear-free.

I am amazed at how relaxed I am, in no hurry to go anywhere or accomplish anything. I am simply enjoying a moment of my life that is unadulterated with doubt, worry, or urgency. Upcoming events and possibilities pass across my mind's eye, but I lack any emotional attachment to them because I have relinquished my need to control their outcomes. The Lord has given me the wisdom to decide how much of myself I can invest in these situations. I do not have to react with surprise or shock or disbelief. However, I can joyfully reply, "Yes, God," to whatever circumstances He chooses to put before me, with full confidence that the outcome, wrapped in His promise to take care of me, will be satisfactory.

I wish I could lie here on the sofa and just write until His return. But alas, there is much to be done. So as I return to the reality of my work, I hope that He will bring me back to this peaceful and soothing state more often. I am grateful for this glimpse into His presence. How did the events in my life get me so far from this amazing and divine oasis of solitude?

Lord, please help me keep my priorities in order. Focus my energy on You, so that I may revisit this wondrous calm in the days to come.

Your Space

Your Space

FEAR-FREE

"Be still, and know that I am God."

Psalms 46:10

"For God has not given us a spirit of fear, but of power, and of love, and of a sound mind."

2 Timothy 1:7

Have you ever had a time of peace in your life that you know had little to do with your own efforts? When? What was the experience?

_____
_____
_____
_____

Do you trust that God will bring you peace during and after your divorce? Has He already begun?

_____
_____
_____
_____

New Beginnings

On my way to the courthouse to get some paperwork signed, I spent the drive thinking about all of the new beginnings ahead of me with the upcoming New Year's celebration. Instead of looking forward to our "first date" anniversary dinner at a Japanese steakhouse, I would be spending New Year's Eve and Day with a friend and her family. I was only days away from becoming single. I would soon reclaim my father's name. There would be lots of errands to run and calls to make. I would begin dating again after almost two decades of being with the same person. (*Do I even know how to date anymore?* I wondered.) My thoughts and feelings were mixed as I parked my car, turned off the CD player, and noticed a knocking sound coming from my engine.

Disheartened, I glanced at the dashboard (there were no lights on), turned off the engine, and climbed out to put more oil in it. This had no effect, and I didn't find any other depleted fluids or apparent problems. I wrapped up my business at the courthouse and headed slowly back to the highway, praying that I could make it to my guardian angel mechanics before they closed. Upon my arrival, I hoped for the best. Their looks, however, prepared me for bad news. I braced myself, since the sting of paying for a new timing belt and tow truck service several months ago was already going to take me another ten months of payments. The guys explained, as gently as they could, that the eighteen-and-a-half-year-old engine was about to have a rod go. My options basically came down to either replacing the engine and gambling that nothing else in the car would go wrong for (hopefully) years or donating the car and buying or leasing another vehicle. I made a quick call to the office to let them know that my couple of hours off had unexpectedly expanded to encompass a new car search for the rest of the afternoon and the following day.

I quietly thanked my friends at the shop and coaxed my car home, speaking to the Lord as I went. I thanked Him for not stranding me on the highway and protecting me from another $100 tow bill. I thanked Him for clearly showing me, as I had prayed, when it was time for me to get another car. I was grateful for getting to my friends' garage and returning home safely. I appreciated that I had already taken time off of work that afternoon, not having any idea that I would need it to compensate for my car's antics. And, in closing, I laughed and thanked Him for giving me a thirty-hour shopping window during the best deal-making day of the year in the auto industry. I tacked on that I was glad to have the support of everyone at the office, all of whom had already picked up their phones to see if anyone they knew could help me find a deal—and fast!

As I set out in my neighbor's car that night to begin the adventure, I prayed, that the Lord would help me to work with all of the eager salespeople and explore whatever car models I could find in order to discover the one He had already chosen for me. I didn't know how I would make the payments, but I trusted Him completely to provide everything I would need, just as He had since I was left alone seven months prior. Having four car models in mind, I swung into "efficiency mode" and hit the nearest car lots. I met several nice gentlemen, but one, in particular, made an impression. After peeking into various models and discussing new versus used and pros versus cons, we headed to his office to entertain the idea of my leasing. However, the first thing he said to me after we sat down was, "Let me ask you a question; are you a Christian?" I smiled and said, "Absolutely!" He smiled too and began talking about his love of the Lord. We eventually got back to the reason for my visit, and he educated me on the various aspects of a lease.

As I left that night (after business hours, no less), I still lacked a specific feeling about any vehicle, but I wasn't panicked either. I arrived home at 11:00p.m.. Tomorrow promised more questions and test drives, but I had a full night's sleep and some serious prayer time between now and then.

By 2:00p.m. the next day (and five dealerships later), I was exhausted and hungry. God had granted me the discernment to know what I *didn't* need, but I still had no specific intuition regarding what He wanted for me. As I got on the highway (in my neighbor's car again), I prayed for extra prompting in the right direction. A moment or two later, my cell phone rang. It was the sweet man from the night before, and he asked me to come back to consider additional discounts on a lease we had discussed. I smiled and said I'd return (accompanied by my drive-thru lunch).

We put our heads together again, and amazing things seemed to happen. The price came down a bit. My credit score had miraculously increased from its previous rating six months ago. The additional debt I had acquired–due to the lack of a joint income for the past three years–was apparently invisible. To my amazement, I decided on a red car, a color that would have been my last choice years ago. I wanted gray interior, but they only had tan for the models on their lot. My agent got online to see if he could track down the vehicle I wanted, and he found only one... at the next nearest dealership in town! Another agent even commented that his locating it was remarkable, since he hadn't heard of anyone else requesting the same combination of colors for that model, nor had he seen a vehicle matching that description. Then I found out that I was approved for no money down, and my first two oil changes were free. The lease I selected included cruise control and other perks that similar models didn't. (Other dealers had offered me the same package but without options and for much more money, even before taxes and tags.) For the next four years, I wouldn't have to worry about carrying around extra gas, oil, radiator fluid, water, or anything else except my emergency roadside kit. Almost every repair would be taken care of–a very new concept for me.

This salesman that God had put before me understood my situation and had done everything he could to empower me in the purchasing process, and on top of it all, the Lord was with me the entire way. His Spirit gave me the confidence to buy this car on faith, knowing in my heart that everything would be paid on time by His hand. I watched my pen sign the contract–a huge event in the absence of my husband and father, but an exciting one in the presence of God, my Provider. As the agent helped detail the car after our drive from the other dealership, my heart glowed, and my face wore a permanent grin.

None of it felt real except for God's grace blessing each step of the way. I had my coworkers, family, friends, church family, and neighbors all praying for my adventure, some of whom even called to check in on my progress during the day. Standing before this profound gift from above, I was humbled. With only rejoicing and amazement in my heart, I felt as if my Father was watching from Heaven with a smile of His own, just for me. I spent New Year's Eve alone but in solitude with the Lord. I was wiped out but grateful for the incredible marathon He had coached me through and the angels He had put in my path along the way. So I enter the new year with tremendous favor from the only love of my life and wonder what else is to come.

Thank you, God. I can't think of anything else to say.

Your Space

Your Space

NEW BEGINNINGS

"But without faith it is impossible to please Him,
for he who comes to God must believe that He is,
and that He is a rewarder of those who diligently seek Him."

Hebrews 11:6

"Jesus answered and said to them,
'Go and tell John the things which you hear and see:
The blind see and the lame walk; the lepers are cleansed and the deaf hear;
the dead are raised up and the poor have the gospel preached to them.
And blessed is he who is not offended because of Me.'"

Matthew 11:4-6

Have you had any profound gifts or changes in your life that seemed to indicate new beginnings? What were they? When did they occur?

_____
_____
_____
_____

Did those gifts or changes help you move forward emotionally? Did they give you hope? How?

_____
_____
_____
_____

The Call

I lay on the sofa, drifting in and out of sleep, my back still very tender from the many injections this morning. Even with the pain medication in my system, I realized my cell phone was ringing on the coffee table, while at the same time knowing from the darkness outside that it was very late. I quickly concluded that whoever it was had urgent news. As I glanced at the caller ID, my heart leaped, then sank. My lawyer's office number was illuminated on the tiny screen, and its purpose was clear. This was the call.

This was the moment in which my ongoing suffering, the "in between" time, and the feelings of abandonment would finally come to a close. When I answered, I knew that one part of my life would end, and another would begin. Once I picked up, things would never be the same again, and the man I once knew as my true love and my best friend would become simply another part of my history. I had begged God to limit my pain; but when the moment finally arrived, I dreaded the reality of it, in spite of the new beginning it represented. My husband had brought me into his life, and now he was dismissing me.

As she acknowledged my 'hello,' my lawyer stated that she had the news that I had been waiting for. *How sad,* I thought, *that I would be waiting for such horrible news. Normally, when someone says that, it is regarding something exciting.*

"Good news. The judge has signed off on your divorce, so it won't be necessary for you to go to court." As she spoke, I sat anticipating the relief, or happiness, or whatever would release me from the mental state I'd been in for so long–waiting for the marathon of the survivor to be over. But it never came, and we quietly hung up a few minutes later.

As I wrapped myself tightly around my pillow and silently cried, the dark sky and twinkling stars my only company, I spoke to the Lord. I told Him that I trusted Him more than anyone else, and I knew in my heart that He wanted me to be happy. Therefore, I would conclude with confidence that I was now one step closer to the blessings He had on the way... peace, contentment, a man, a family, and a new me who would have much to contribute in the eyes of my Father, Husband, and Friend. I realized that I had become completely available to do the important things He had called me to do, with all of my heart, energy, and attention, which was where I should have been a long time ago.

Your Space

THE CALL

"For with God nothing will be impossible."

Luke 1:37

What key moments do you remember from your stages of divorce?

_____
_____
_____
_____

What set those moments apart from the others? Did you have certain expectations? Were they fulfilled?

_____
_____
_____
_____

✥

The Letter

I just knew it was sitting in the mailbox waiting for me. I opened the small metal door and saw the thick envelope with my maiden name typed on the front. It was all I could to do reach in and retrieve the stack of bills with my divorce paperwork resting on top. I dragged myself into the house and called my neighbor. I needed a close friend to come and buffer me from the harshness of final decree–the pronouncement of my love and passion for a single man being put aside by the legal system.

As she read the impartial and extensive legal jargon, I sobbed. "...ordered and decreed by the Court that the marriage contract... dissolved as fully and effectually as if no such contract had ever been made...." The moment felt surreal. After all of the grieving I'd already gone through, I expected a sense of relief, but instead I experienced what felt like death. It took several hours for me to move past the letter's fresh, sharp cut to my heart, but I eventually left the house to tackle the task of changing my name on my bank and business accounts. When I returned, I called every utility company and updated those accounts as well. I began to reflect on how proud I am of my father's name, and I thanked the Lord for the stable and supportive presence that both of my parents had been throughout my life. I knew that this phase would eventually end, and the scars that were left would heal and fade away, leaving my soul fresh and renewed. I just hoped that time would be soon.

The next morning I felt rejuvenated and moved from place to place in the favor of God–no lines to wait in, no problems or issues, no worries as I took back a semblance of control in my life. As I neared the end of my 'to-do list, I felt a sense of relief and anticipation. I had been hanging on for so long, hoping for a miracle but having to accept a different reality. No more.

I was now plowing ahead, seeking the Lord's work, and trusting in His path for me. The effort, time, and love that was once lost would now be put into something hopeful and promising.

Just lead me, Lord, and I will follow.

Your Space

Your Space

THE LETTER

*"Jesus said to him, **'Thomas, because you have seen Me, you have believed. Blessed are those who have not seen and yet have believed.'**"*

John 20:29

"The LORD is my shepherd; I shall not want. He makes me to lie down in green pastures; He leads me beside the still waters. He restores my soul; He leads me in the paths of righteousness For His name's sake. Yea, though I walk through the valley of the shadow of death, I will fear no evil; For You are with me; Your rod and Your staff, they comfort me. You prepare a table before me in the presence of my enemies; You anoint my head with oil; My cup runs over. Surely goodness and mercy shall follow me All the days of my life; And I will dwell in the house of the LORD Forever."

Psalms 23:1-6

Can you remember a time when you felt like your faith was the only thing holding you up? When was it? What happened?

_____
_____
_____
_____

Looking back, did surviving such a trial give you encouragement when you hit new challenges?

_____
_____
_____
_____

Victimhood

Okay, so I was the victim of a divorce. Although the process has been extremely painful, I am now grateful for the circumstances around my particular situation. I had no children to whom I had to explain what divorce was. I was not the victim of physical abuse. I had a stable environment at home that allowed me to grieve, pray, and write. My family was on call for all of my needs. I had amazing friends, coworkers, and neighbors who showered me with blessings of all kinds. I had a spiritual community in my church and Bible Study groups who prayed for, listened to, and supported me. I had access to two counselors (through work and church) who guided me through the process and provided clarity from independent parties' perspectives. My attorney knew both my ex-husband and me, so he was comfortable with my hiring her. All in all, the Lord provided as much TLC as He could for me, and I am so appreciative of His generosity.

Regardless of the positive aspects that I look back and see, there is one very important step that facilitated my healing by leaps and bounds: I decided that being a victim of divorce would no longer define me. I stopped bringing it up in conversation. I stopped blaming it for any hardships I was having. I refused to use it as an excuse to avoid interacting with others. I would not mention it to gain any benefits. I stopped blaming any shortcoming on the fact that a man had left me.

Now obviously my situation might have been simple compared to most, but attitude is everything when overcoming trauma. I let go of the "poor me" face and perspective. I decided to give more to those around me instead of hoping for more from them. I introduce myself as single (because I *am*). "Divorced" really only counts on your taxes and legal documents, so think about it–how do you use the word? "Divorced" *does not* mean damaged goods. The dynamics in your situation may vary, but I urge you to adopt the perspective that regardless of your circumstances, God will do a new work in you, if you let Him. Don't cleave to the pain, anger, resentment, and victim mentality longer than is healthy. Grieve, scream, get counseling, or do whatever it takes, then MOVE ON. All of that internal strife will only fester and eventually reveal a person you won't recognize. If support groups help you process the experience, then go, but do not stay so long that you come out feeling worse than when you went in. Focus on people and activities that bring you up and avoid those that bring you down. Seek balance in your life, and let it start with God's wisdom and will for you. Take charge of the phenomenal man or woman of God you were created to be. Don't let someone else's attack on your mind and heart (or worse) control you for the rest of your life. It's *your* choice.

Victimhood is an okay neighborhood to visit, but don't you dare buy a house and get comfortable there! The Lord has too much for us to do and too much happiness, success, and peace reserved for us that we will miss if we remain victims.

Thank you, Lord, for sending me everything I needed to recover and focus on what is important to You in my life. I hope You will help the many, many others who are struggling with the same issues and pain as I have these last several years, so that they find the healing they need as well.

Your Space

VICTIMHOOD

*"But the LORD said to Samuel, 'Do not look at his appearance
or at the height of his stature, because I have refused him.
For the LORD does not see as man sees; or man looks at the outward appearance,
but the LORD looks at the heart.'"*

I Samuel 16:7

What do you say to people about your divorce? Is it the first thing you bring up in conversation?

_____
_____
_____
_____

Does discussing it make you feel better or worse? What can you do to help yourself move on?

_____
_____
_____
_____

My Valentine's Date

I stood beside the 60-percent-off clearance rack looking for a present for Mom. It was Valentine's Day, and her birthday was only three days away. As I flipped through the hangers and plucked out the perfect top for YM (affectionately known as *Your Mama* in her emails), I glanced down to see another shirt that caught my eye with its sparkles and stretchy fabric. Struggling to justify the purchase of this playful top (and possibly the greatly discounted black jacket next to it), I began to rationalize how to buy such items when I really couldn't afford them... even on sale.

I had stood there for only a moment when a thought popped into my head. I glanced up toward the ceiling and asked, "Lord, would you like to be my date tonight?" Although this night was normally advertised for friends and lovers, I didn't care. I was physically alone this year, but I wouldn't really be alone. As the thought of this new date night grew on me, I became excited and began celebrating in advance by scooping up my items, trying them on, and heading to the counter to pay for the gifts for Mom and me. I couldn't contain my giggling as the special evening took form in my mind. I went to the grocery store and bought the fixings for my favorite spaetzles dish, salad, and dessert.

When I got home, I prepared all of the dishes and a festive drink. Once the food was ready, I collected all of the fresh flowers that I'd staged around the house and gently arranged them on the kitchen table. I pulled out numerous candles from the pantry and set the table with a brand new glass, plate, napkin, and place mat. When I was satisfied that all was ready (ignoring the dishes and cutting boards strewn across my counter tops, of course), I headed upstairs to shower and change, giving my preparation the same time and attention as I would for a date. Forty-five minutes later, with my make-up done, hair styled, and the new outfit on, I returned to the kitchen table for my date. With the candles lit and the other lights turned off, I spent almost half an hour with my Lord, thanking, praising, and simply talking with Him. I enjoyed our meal thoroughly, and it struck me how content I felt when I finished eating and eventually blew out the candles. He was the perfect date. He was right on time, provided for all of the meal's content and décor, listened with a kind ear, thought I was beautiful (even though I'd forgotten my lipstick), had waited patiently, wasn't picky about the menu, and gave me His undivided love and attention.

I had dreaded this manufactured holiday and its reminder of my single status, yet He moved in my heart and created fun, play, and anticipation of an experience more fulfilling than I could have hoped for. I don't think I'll ever look at Valentine's Day the same way again.

Your Space

MY VALENTINE'S DATE

*"Blessed is every one who fears the LORD, Who walks in His ways.
When you eat the labor of your hands, You shall be happy,
and it shall be well with you. Your wife shall be like a fruitful vine
In the very heart of your house, Your children are like olive plants
All around your table. Behold, thus shall the man be blessed
Who fears the LORD."*

Psalms 128:1-4

What have you done for yourself lately (could be a purchase, travel, event, etc.)?

_____
_____
_____
_____

Did you involve the Lord in your plans? How? Are you aware of His desire for you to be happy?

_____
_____
_____
_____

Another Loss

I have been coasting along on an amazing wave of grace for the last ten days. It started with my date with God, continued with awesome prayer and inspiration time, included unexpectedly inheriting a laptop (!), and all the while I was getting messages from the Lord to ask, ask, ask for things... though I wasn't sure for what or why or when.

I was feeling lighthearted at work as I sat at my desk and started knocking out my list of daily responsibilities. After only thirty minutes or so, my manager asked if I "had a second" to come and see him. The words didn't have the usual ring that his other requests normally did, and as I walked to his office, I felt like something was wrong. He closed the door, which was the usual for some topics, but he seemed strained as he sat down behind his desk. My gut wrenched, and my heart fell into my stomach. Something was *very* wrong.

He looked me squarely, but gently, in the eye and calmly dialed a phone number. As a man on speakerphone picked up on the other end, my boss began by saying, "As you know, we've had a lot of restructuring this past year... ."

The words smacked me full force across the cheek. I immediately knew I was being laid off. As I listened to their explanations and prepared statements about my options, my thoughts were hard to control. *Oh, God,* I thought. *What am I supposed to do with the house? Medical care? All of life's other details?* Then, my mind flew to my dear friend and coworker who was the other office secretary and a thirty-two year veteran of the company. *What would **she** do?!?! This cannot be happening!*

The tears were streaming down my face. I remember hearing a few cursory comments from the Human Resources representative on the speakerphone before he ended the call. I felt hot, my face was a sticky mess, and my heart pounded in my ears. Although my manager explained the possibility of being selected for a few of the new positions that might become available, I couldn't focus my attention on him. His face held a sadness deeper than any I'd seen in four years of our working together, and he still had to tell my friend that her career would also be ending. My heart ached.

He walked around from behind his desk and placed his hand gently on my shoulder, simply standing beside me while I wept and quietly telling me he was sorry, over and over again. I'm not sure if I was crying more for me or for my friend, but my boss told me that if I needed to go home, I could. So I walked hurriedly to my desk, grabbed my keys, and left the office. As I passed my friend next to the mailbox in the parking lot, I couldn't answer her questioning gaze or concerned words with anything other than "I really can't talk about it," my face still glistening with my tears.

When I got home, I sat on the floor, pulled my knees up, and let it rip. I wailed and cried out to the Lord for help, for what seemed like the millionth time. I saw pictures of myself losing my house, my car, my possessions, and my sanity. I felt completely vulnerable and asked God to protect me. The more I spoke to Him, the farther away my fear moved, and the calmer I became. The last nine months of losses had overwhelmed me: husband, dogs, other relationships, car, job... *and the house is only a matter of time,* I thought. The lay-off had blindsided me, and all of the suffering that had come before it only compounded its power.

A few minutes later the phone rang–it was my friend from work. She, too, was devastated. I invited her to come over, and we sat together and grieved. Eventually, we started to plan, and I told her we could build her an incredible résumé for her new job-hunting endeavors. I mentally gave mine a thought or two, but my greatest concern was for her and her family. How would this affect them?

After she returned to work so that she wouldn't get behind, I spent the remainder of the day working on my own resume and references, preparing myself for the employment applications that were suddenly part of my future, both with my company and others. I worked on what I could control and trusted Him with everything else.

Tomorrow, I will go into the office and apply for the job, and I will wait for His answer for the next step in my life.

Please take my anxiety away, Lord. It does me no good to worry about what may or may not happen, since there is little I can do to battle what I cannot see. Please make a way for me.

Your Space

ANOTHER LOSS

"Nebuchadnezzar spoke, saying, 'Blessed be the God of Shadrach, Meshach, and Abed-Nego, who sent His Angel and delivered His servants who trusted in Him, and they have frustrated the king's word, and yielded their bodies, that they should not serve nor worship any god except their own God!'"

Daniel 3:28

"If ye abide in me, and my Word lives in you, then ye shall ask what you will, and it shall be done unto you."

John 15:7 (KJV)

Other than the different aspects of divorce, have you had any other experiences that you felt were out of your control? What were they?

_____

_____

_____

_____

Does the divorce make you feel like other events impact your life much more drastically than they actually do? How do you cope with the ongoing stressors?

_____

_____

_____

_____

Grieving

Although my schedule has been typical this month, I have felt extremely tired, moreso than usual. My friend said that I may be experiencing grief's impact on my body. I have asked the Lord for healing, but my friend thinks that I may be overloaded and need to take some time off. So after twelve days of house- and pet-sitting for some friends who went out of town, I took the weekend off to tend to myself.

The sofa has been my home for thirty-six hours, and I have only left it to shower and pick up a pizza. (I even skipped going to church this morning because I didn't think I would have the energy to effectively perform my volunteer duties.) God blessed me with several naps yesterday and today, and He included a ten-hour window of regular sleep last night. I've spent time praying and reading the Word. While I was reading another book, I started crying and didn't stop for almost an hour. My sobs first came out of grief, from my rejected love for him. But as time passed, my tears were for deeper pains that lingered in the recesses of my soul–pains that had no specific memory or emotion to identify them–pains that were so old they blended together in a pool of darkness that was pulled from the inside of my being and expelled from my body. It kept coming out, like God had allowed me to become so tired that I wouldn't be able to keep Him from digging up the dregs of my history and banishing them from my being.

Exhausted again, I fell asleep and have just now awoken from another nap. I am grateful for the release and rest. With this weekend of acknowledging my fatigue, I have moved forward another step in my healing. But I pray that God will continue to trigger it, because I want it gone–all of it. Though it has been a hurdle to my footsteps, the process has been medicine for my heart.

Lord, please heal my soul so that it will be fresh for what lies ahead of me.

Your Space

Your Space

GRIEVING

"Have mercy on me, O LORD, for I am in trouble;
My eye wastes away with grief, Yes, my soul and my body!"

Psalms 31:9

"I can do all things through Christ who strengthens me."

Philippians 4:13

Do you have a safe place where you can grieve the loss of your marriage? Where?

_____
_____
_____
_____

Has the Lord provided any relief from your mourning? Whom do you lean on for support when you are hurting?

_____
_____
_____
_____

The Shift

I didn't realize the full impact of my grieving experience until this morning. Until then, I had only felt fatigue and the slight swelling around my eyes. But that was before IT happened.

I was sitting at my desk when an email popped into my inbox. Since I receive so many of them each day, I reflexively double-clicked on the preview in the bottom right-hand corner of my desktop to open it. The message was from him. I thought it was odd that he would contact me, since the divorce was final months ago. Before my weekend of rest and healing, my brain would have immediately swung into a defensive mode, and I would have sounded the alarm to throw a wall of protection up around my heart. Instead, the calmness of God was within me. I glanced at the single line of text that read "Is it true that you will be laid off this week?"

The old me would have reacted with thoughts similar to "Like you really care!" or "It's not your problem anymore," followed by a quick trip to the bathroom for a meltdown. However, the heart that answered him was not from that person. Suddenly, it seemed perfectly normal to respond to his question with simple facts and honesty. I immediately typed out a reply detailing the events and telling him that I had been rehired into one of the few positions left in the area. I concluded with the comment that I was going to be okay, and he no longer needed to worry about me. After sending my reply, I had to take a moment to figure out who I was and what God had done with my other self, who had mysteriously disappeared. In a way I was shocked with my own reaction, or I should say lack thereof. I soaked in this novel sensation, one of steadiness and tranquility. A spiritual shift had occurred.

The strangest part about the few emails that bounced between us is that they failed to jerk my heartstrings like they once did. I was able to react objectively to someone who used to affect the very core of my spirit with his words and presence. Suddenly, I felt willing and able to meet with him face-to-face, and I realized that there were some things I needed to tell him in person before he decided to leave the area. As we finished our notes, I basked in the glow of the freedom I was experiencing, now that the Lord had removed the chains of emotional bondage. He had disconnected me from my ex-husband in such a powerful way, and I wouldn't have even known it had this email conversation failed to take place. What timing! He had prepared me in advance for things He knew were coming.

The rest of the day's activities faded to the back of my mind. The happiness that accompanied my newfound freedom enveloped me. I had struggled to release many things over the course of the last few years, and God took me through the final steps that I was not equipped to tackle on my own. Now that He had moved me into a fresh phase of life, I knew that I wouldn't and couldn't ever return to the former. What a relief! I was safely established in the comfort of being completely emotionally detached from my ex-husband. God had mended my broken heart and given me peace.

Thank you, Lord, for this phenomenal healing.

Your Space

THE SHIFT

"I will stand my watch And set myself on the rampart,
And watch to see what He will say to me, And what I will answer when I am corrected.
Then the LORD answered me and said: Write the vision And make it plain on tablets,
That he may run who reads it. For the vision is yet for an appointed time;
But at the end it will speak, and it will not lie. Though it tarries, wait for it;
Because it will surely come, It will not tarry."

Habakkuk 2:1-3

Think back to a time when you were recovering from a serious injury. At what point did you realize that you had reached a significant level of healing?

_____

_____

_____

_____

Have your heart and spirit experienced complete healing yet? If not, do you feel it moving closer to you?

_____

_____

_____

_____

Have you asked God to intercede and grant you the spiritual mending that your soul desires? If not, why not?

_____

_____

_____

_____

Trust

In my late teens and early twenties, I dreamed about what the future would hold. I wanted to teach and touch the lives of the young. Along the way, I also wanted to find "him" and enjoy the world with someone who loved me. My heart yearned for a large family, in which we could savor God's blessing of each other and our children. I hoped for enough prosperity that I could homeschool our kids. I imagined pets that would give our family their unconditional love. And, of course, my hopes also included the joy of sharing our family with my parents and grandparents. Above all, I wanted to live in such a way that it would be pleasing to God.

Now it's easy to say that you trust God, especially when life seems to be running smoothly. "Yes, I'm a Christian," I've told many people. "I believe that God can turn all things into something good for His purposes. Even when we have no idea what or when or why or how such horrible life events could glorify Him, He will do it." The strength of that trust isn't tested until you hit a bump or pothole in the road. Then you are forced to examine whether that trust really exists or if it is just a sign of token faith.

Fast-forward fifteen years... where my life appears to have come to a crashing halt. Yes, I did become a teacher and (hopefully) was able to affect many kids' lives in a positive way during my nine years in the classroom. However, I left teaching when the growing list of certifications that were required became overwhelming. I trusted that God needed my energy elsewhere and stepped out of my teaching comfort zone in faith. The rest isn't so cut-and-dried. I found who I thought was "the one," only to find out seventeen years later that he decided he wasn't. Consequently, we had no family, but we did have a few four-legged children, two of which we had to put down, and the third now lives with him.

So my house is devoid of animal affection, and it will probably stay that way, since the divorce has forced me to put the house on the market. As of this writing, I am a secretary who was laid off four months ago and then hired back. I have no idea what the Lord has in store for me. All I know is that He wants me to write. So I do and trust in Him to guide me the rest of the way–in my career, relationships, health, and happiness.

Am I disappointed with where I am in my life, compared with past dreams? Absolutely!

Do I find it depressing to have invested so much time and energy into something that has been tossed aside? Certainly!

But even though I feel lacking, I wouldn't have the relationship with the Lord that I have now except as a result of my life's circumstances. I wouldn't trade it for anything... not even for the fulfillment of what I thought I wanted and needed in my life.

I also know from His Word that He can bring me the desires of my heart (and then some) at any moment. All I can do is try to be obedient to His expectations and believe that He will fill my heart with amazing hopes and dreams again. I trust His Word to be truth, even when I feel like my face has been in the dirt so long that I have gravel stuck between my teeth.

Instead of feeling sorry for myself, I choose to anticipate the excitement of people, places, events, and enriched faith yet to come–for He has told me that "all things work together for good for those who love God" (Romans 8:28), and I trust Him to use the fallout from my life to do just that–to create something beautiful in His own way.

Your Space

TRUST

"As for God, His way is perfect; The word of the LORD is proven; He is a shield to all who trust in Him."

2 Samuel 22:31

"'For I will surely deliver you, and you shall not fall by the sword; but your life shall be as a prize to you, because you have put your trust in Me,' says the LORD."

Jeremiah 39:18

Trust is a huge issue in relationships. How has your divorce affected your sense of trust? Do you find yourself second-guessing where you stand with other people?

_____
_____
_____
_____

Do you trust the Lord? Has your divorce changed your level of trust in God? Has it gotten stronger or weaker? Why?

_____
_____
_____
_____

Today

It's been exactly one hundred and fifty days since the divorce was finalized, and I look back at how the Lord has done incredible things in my life over the last couple of years. He has directed me to write a second book about our experiences together through the divorce. (The first was a devotional called *Walking Faith Forward,* published in 2007.) He has healed me in many ways. He has brought calm back into my being and taken fear completely away. He has put an abundance of friends in my journey to help and encourage me, and often I find they need my encouragement as well. He has raised up an amazing church home for me. He has kept a roof over my head, food on my table, and clothes on my back. He has given me transportation and a job with which I can support myself. He has blessed me with a realtor who has been loyal and faithful through the challenges of the process of selling a house during a divorce. He is bringing unexpected joy back into my life. He has remade me into someone new, having a clean slate and much potential. He has taught me how to ask and to receive. He has forgiven me, in His great mercy, for all that has passed and will be no more. He has inspired ministry in my heart and made it manifest in my life. He has protected and comforted me through the storm.

He has listened to my thoughts, prayers, and tears, answering each with His wisdom and compassion. He has been gradually healing my back so that one day I will feel like I've returned to a "normal" activity level. He has helped me to rediscover laughter. He has given me a self-image that is one of beauty and contentment... just as I am... just as He created me to be. He has provided me with even more abilities and a heightened desire to do whatever I can for others. He has given me eyes to see the fullness of my life instead of dwelling on what I think is missing. He has given me peace in the lack of knowledge about where my life is going or what will happen next. He has been the only absolute I have ever known–the rock upon which I place all of my hopes, dreams, and most importantly, faith.

Thank you, Lord, for bringing me to today.

Your Space

Your Space

TODAY

"The law of the LORD is perfect, converting the soul; The testimony of the LORD is sure, making wise the simple; The statutes of the LORD are right, rejoicing the heart; The commandment of the LORD is pure, enlightening the eyes; The fear of the LORD is clean, enduring forever; The judgments of the LORD are true and righteous altogether. More to be desired are they than gold, Yea, than much fine gold; Sweeter also than honey and the honeycomb."

Psalms 19:7-10

Have you seen steps that God has already taken on your behalf during the divorce process? What were they? If not, have you asked Him (being specific) for help?

_____
_____
_____
_____

Make a list of things with which you need the most assistance from the Lord. These may be issues that are yours alone or those that involve other people. Regardless, bring them before God, lay them at His feet, and let them go. He wants to carry them for you.

_____
_____
_____
_____

The Journey Continues...

As I close the window of this part of my life, I feel God continuing to put even more distance between the divorce and me. The only thoughts that remain for him are mostly of sadness and loneliness, not for me personally, but because I believe he is still experiencing those deep and painful feelings.

On the other hand, the Lord has filled my life with the peace that only a fresh spiritual start can bring. I've made new friends, gone on adventures (both with friends and on my own), pursued personal interests (old and new), stepped out into an ever-deepening faith, and embraced fun experiences that I once would have let pass by. I have even discovered the art of self-indulgence on occasion, with a gift here and there just for me–just because.

I now make plans instead of waiting to chart my course according to my significant other's schedule. (Previously, I usually made temporary plans that were based on his commitments and interests in an effort to spend time together.) In the morning I wake with gratefulness in my heart for the hope and promises of the day, instead of insecurity from not knowing what is to come. I no longer have to worry about creating solutions for the "what ifs" that I used to fear.

I appreciate the love and affection of my family and friends much more, because I've realized that there are no guarantees in relationships–only choices. I anticipate the amazing steps that God will take in my life to fulfill my desires, little or big. I am a youngster again, standing on the edge of the high dive, waiting for the Lord's call to coax me into the deep and invigorating waters that will refresh my spirit and take me into the next season of my life. I am ready and listening, Lord. I trust You.

Your Space

Your Space

THE JOURNEY CONTINUES

"For I know the plans I have for you, declares the LORD... "
                                                    Jeremiah 29:11 (ESV)

What hopes and dreams do you have for today and your future?

_____
_____
_____
_____

Is the Lord an important part of your plans? Why or why not?

_____
_____
_____
_____

What step you can take today to help you move forward on your journey?

_____
_____
_____
_____

Epilogue

I encourage anyone who is having difficulty with his or her marriage or going through a divorce to pursue as many healthy forms of support as possible. Seek out people who can offer professional guidance, personal encouragement, and consistent assistance with everyday "baby steps" that will move you to and through the healing process. Victims in relationships are only victims by choice. Although others have the ability to take away your options, only you can allow the transition from strong individual to victim. It is my desire that you will persevere through your own situation and maintain a sense of dignity during the process. I wish you well on your journey.

www.ingramcontent.com/pod-product-compliance
Lightning Source LLC
Chambersburg PA
CBHW040000080526
44586CB00027B/2832